EXCEL 2

The Must-Have Guide to Master Microsoft Excel | From Beginner to Pro in less than 7 days | Step-by-step Formulas and Functions with tutorials and illustrations

By
Gil B. Dreher

Dear Reader,

Thanks for choosing my book. **Welcome to the Excel 2022.**

My name is Gil B. Dreher, and I am an engineer and a professional programmer, and app developer.

I am a professional programmer and app developer. Over the years I have developed knowledge and skills in a lot of software and programs, just like Excel.

From this passion, this handy guide was born, to enable anyone to learn how to use this fantastic tool.

I hope this course can quickly and easily teach you how to become a true Excel pro.

Don't forget to download your bonuses, a practical 6-hour video course, and many ready-to-use templates.

You'll find how to download them at the end of the book.

Positive reviews from wonderful customers like you help others feel confident about choosing this Guide. Sharing your happy experience will be greatly appreciated!

 scan the Qr Code to leave your review on Amazon (US)   scan the Qr Code to leave your review on Amazon (UK)

Contents

Introduction 5

Chapter 1: What Is Microsoft Excel? 6
1.1 What Is Excel Used For? 6
1.2 History and Future of MS Excel 7
1.3 Present Day Microsoft Excel 7
1.4 The Future of Excel 7
1.5 Data Functions, Formulas, and Shortcuts 7

Chapter 2: Why Learn Excel 2022? 8
2.1 Why Use Formulas? 8
2.2 How to Add Text to a Cell in Excel? 9
2.3 Excel Multiplication Formula 10
2.4 IF Function of Excel 11
2.5 Excel Array Formula 12
2.6 Average Formulas in Excel 13
2.7 Percentage Formula in Excel 14
2.8 Excel Variance Formula 15

Chapter 3: Basic Excel Formulas 19
3.1 Five Time-Saving Ways to Insert Data into Excel 19
3.2 Basic Formulas for Excel Workflow 20
3.3 Excel Shortcuts 22

Chapter 4: Ten Advanced Excel Formulas 25
4.1 Advanced Formulas 25
4.2 Excel Formulas: The Cheat Sheet 29

Chapter 5: Modifying the Worksheet 31
5.1 Moving to a Specific Cell 31
5.2 Adding a Row & Column 31
5.3 Shortcut Menu 31
5.4 Resizing a Column and Row 32
5.5 Selecting a Cell 32
5.6 Cutting, Copying, and Pasting Cells 33
5.7 Keeping Headings Visible 35

Chapter 6: Five Ways Excel Can Improve Productivity During Your Work from Home 36
6.1 Processing Large Amounts of Data 36
6.2 Utilizing Fill Handles 36
6.3 Examining Formulas All at Once 36
6.4 Leverage the Goal Seek Formula 36
6.5 Automate Recurring Responsibilities With VBA 36
6.6 Best Excel Templates to Increase or Boost Your Productivity 36

Chapter 7: Relative, Absolute, and Mixed Cell References in Excel 37
7.1 What Are Relative Cell References in Excel? 37
7.2 Excel Absolute Cell Reference 38
7.3 What Are Mixed Cell References in Excel? 39
7.4 How to Change the Reference from Relative to Absolute (or Mixed)? 40
7.5 Multiplication Table Utilizing Mixed References 40
7.6 Multiplication Table Utilizing an Array Formula 42
7.7 Create the Multiplication Table in Google Sheets 42

Chapter 8: MS Excel: The WORKDAY.INTL Function 42
8.1 How to Use a WORKDAY.INTL Function in Excel? 42
8.2 MS Excel: The RANDBETWEEN Function 47
8.3 Excel RAND Function 47

Chapter 9: MS Excel: The VLOOKUP Function 49
9.1 How to Use VLOOKUP in Excel? 49
9.2 VLOOKUP in Financial Modeling and Financial Analysis 50
9.3 Things to remember about the VLOOKUP Function 50
9.4 MS Excel: the HLOOKUP Function 50
9.5 Tips for HLOOKUP Function 51

Chapter 10: MS Excel: the TRANSPOSE Function (WS) 51
10.1 How to use the TRANSPOSE Function in Excel? 51
10.2 MS Excel: The COUNTBLANK Function 52

Chapter 11: Convert Numbers into Words 53
11.1 How to Convert the Number into Words? 53

Chapter 12: Excel Data Entry Form 57
12.1 Data Entry Form in Excel 58
12.2 Parts of the Data Entry Form 59
12.3 Creating Another New Entry 60
12.4 Navigating Through the Existing Records 60
12.5 Deleting a Record 63
12.6 Restricting Data Entry Based on Rules 63

Gil B. Dreher

12.7 How to Use the Data Validation Along with the Data Entry Form?...65
12.8 How to Open the Data Entry Form With VBA?..65

Chapter 13: Excel Valuation Modeling **69**

13.1 Valuation Modeling 69
13.2 Why Perform Valuation Modeling in Excel? 69
13.3 How to Execute Excel Valuation Modeling?...69
13.4 Jobs That Perform Valuation Modeling in Excel 70
13.5 Main Valuation Methods 70

Chapter 14: Mathematical and Statistical Functions **71**

14.1 Excel Math Functions 71
14.2 Statistical Functions in Excel 77

Chapter 15: Use of Five Advanced Excel Pivot Table Techniques **79**

15.1 Slicers...80
15.2 Timelines 81
15.3 Tabular View 82
15.4 Calculated Fields 83
15.5 Recommended Pivot Tables 84

Chapter 16: Create Charts in Excel: Types and Examples **85**

16.1 Types of Charts 85
16.2 How to Insert Charts in Excel? 86
16.3 Top Five Excel Graph and Chart Best Practices 87
16.4 How You can Chart Data in Excel 88

Chapter 17: Excel Table **100**

17.1 How to Create a Table in Excel?...101
17.2 How to Make a Table with a Selected Style? 103
17.3 How to Name a Table in Excel? 104
17.4 How to Use Tables in Excel? 105
17.5 How to Sort a Table in Excel?..106
17.6 How to Extend a Table in Excel? 107
17.7 How to Remove the Table Formatting? 108
17.8 How to Remove a Table in Excel? 109

Chapter 18: How to Become a Data Analyst in 2022? **110**

18.1 What Does a Data Analyst Do? 110
18.2 What Is Data Analytics?...110
18.3 Data Analyst Qualifications 110
18.4 Data Analyst Responsibilities 110
18.5 What Tools Do Data Analysts Use? 110
18.6 Data Analysts Job 111
18.7 Data Analyst Salary 111
18.8 Data Analyst Career Path 111
18.9 Is Data Analysis a Growing Field?..111
18.10 How to Become a Data Analyst with No Experience?..111

Chapter 19: What Skills Should You look for while hiring an Excel Expert? **111**

19.1 For Entry Level/Administrative Jobs...112
19.2 For Senior Level / Excel Specialists / Excel Experts...112
19.3 Business Analyst Excel Skills 112
19.4 Data Analyst Excel Skills 113
19.5 Auditor Excel Skills 113
19.6 Seven Tips to Improve Basic MS Excel Skills...113

BONUS **115**

Conclusion...**116**

Introduction

Digital transformation is revolutionizing the educational and professional sectors, requiring constant updating and increasingly advanced digital skills.
To enter the job market or pursue a university career, it is important to master several technologies considered essential nowadays, including the tools of the Office package.

In particular, Microsoft Excel is an indispensable program in many professional fields. It is essential to develop adequate basic training and some advanced skills by aligning with the needs of business and academia.
Excel is one of the world's most well-known and widely used programs, through which a range of tasks can be performed, including making spreadsheets, and charts, creating formulas and statistical data and coordinating teams' work efficiently.

The software was launched on the market in 1985 as a solution aimed primarily at enterprises and the business sector, however, it was quickly adopted in academia and universities.

The widespread use of this tool has made Excel skills a prerequisite in recruiting activities, enhancing the abilities of candidates who demonstrate proficiency in the functionality of this software.
The evolution of digital technologies, with the introduction of more sophisticated systems for Big Data analysis and the use of artificial intelligence programs, has not reduced the importance of Microsoft Excel for companies, which remains essential in business and education.

The potential of Excel is numerous; in fact, it makes available within the same program so many functions that can integrate seamlessly with each other and with other applications. In detail, the tool from the house of Microsoft allows you to build custom spreadsheets, simplify accounting, make any chart, monitor inventories and orders, create customized schedules and worksheets to plan work objectives.
In addition, with this program, you can make checklists, administer complex projects, implement accurate calendars, manage contacts and even records of various kinds. The benefits of Excel are diverse; in fact, the software helps save time, foster collaboration, enhance digitization, and increase productivity. Not least, it allows you to share resources, create custom forms and analyze data accurately.

Knowing how to master excel and all its functions can not only help you in the working world but also has a great deal of utility on a personal level., for example, family budget, personal accounting, management and planning of everything in your life.
Microsoft Excel will help you manipulate, monitor, and evaluate results, making more informed decisions and saving time and money. So now is the time to embark on your journey into the fantastic world of Excel to learn from scratch or improve your current knowledge of this beneficial program.

Enjoy

Chapter 1: What Is Microsoft Excel?

With the assistance of Microsoft Excel, one can save, organize, and analyze data. Despite the application's brief history, it has gained widespread popularity among office computer users (1985 release date). Excel gurus might be valuable for any business activity, irrespective of their operating sector.

Excel has become an essential component of company processes worldwide, whether it is for analyzing stocks or issuers, obtaining funding, or keeping customer sales lists updated.

You can alter data that has been put into a spreadsheet using Microsoft Excel. Excel's advanced analytical and computational skills have made it one of the most popular choices among professionals working in finance and accounting.

Microsoft Excel has the capability of locating trends and generating categories that are pertinent to the data.

Excel can execute functions related to human resources, such as classifying hours worked and organizing personnel profiles and expenses. This enables businesses to better understand the composition and operations of their staff. Using pivot tables, a graph is created that summarizes the data from the worksheet.

1.1 What Is Excel Used For?

Finance & Accounting

Spreadsheets in Excel are helpful in finance, particularly in accounting and financial services. Before 1983, financial professionals would spend weeks manually conducting complicated computations, such as those seen in Lotus 1-2-3. Excel has made it feasible to conduct complex modeling in a couple of minutes rather than hours.

In any large corporate office's accounting and finance departments, Excel spreadsheets are used to crunch data, describe financial consequences, and develop budgets, predictions, and plans that are employed in making important business choices.

Excel's fundamental IF operations, which include addition, subtraction, multiplication, and division, are well-known. However, the advanced IF functions that are accessible via the use of INDEX-MATCH-MATCH, VLOOKUP, and pivot tables offer a world of possibilities.

Marketing & Product Management

Even though marketing and product managers rely on their financial institutions to do the hard work regarding financial research, spreadsheets may help them manage their sales staff and plan future marketing plans based on previous performance.

Utilizing a pivot table, you can rapidly generate a summary of the customers and sales data by class by using a simple drag-and-drop interface.

Human Resources Planning

Exporting payroll and personnel data to Excel gives companies a better picture of how their workforce is broken up by pay level or job function and assists them in seeing trends. Payroll and personnel data may be managed using various programs, including Oracle, SAP, and QuickBooks.

Due to an error that cannot be undone, Excel will display erroneous results for all dates before March 1, 1900.

Excel may be used to analyze a huge spreadsheet, including employee data, to determine the source of the expenditures and the most effective way to plan for and administer them in the future.

You Can Do Anything with a Spreadsheet

Excel's business applications are endless. The following are some examples:

- Excel is useful for keeping tabs on things like RSVPs and costs when planning an outing for a baseball club.
- Excel generates revenue growth predictions for new products based on estimations obtained from existing and prospective new consumers.
- To organize your website's publication calendar, you might use a spreadsheet.
- Creating a budget for a small product may be as easy as entering all the costs into a spreadsheet, which you can then keep up to date every month, and then generating a graph to show how close your product is to stay within its allotted budget for each category. This is all that is required to create a budget for a small product.
- It is possible to determine the amount of a customer's discount by considering the monthly volume of their purchases.
- The money generated by clients may be broken down by product, allowing users to determine the areas in which they can strengthen their relationships with those consumers.
- Make use of more complex equations, such as the Sharpe ratio.
- Excel was the first program to have the toolbar in its interface.

Excel Is Not Going Anywhere

Excel will continue to be a cornerstone if firms utilize it for various jobs and purposes, including IT projects and office picnics.

Excel expertise is now required of a significant number of office workers, and those who have refined their Excel skills may be in a better position to grow in their professions and take on more responsibilities. Excel's strength cannot be denied; however, the program cannot do every function on its own. Excel's full functionality can only be unlocked by an expert user who is familiar with the program and knows how to make the most of its capabilities.

What Is Microsoft Excel and How Is It Used in Business?

Spreadsheet software such as Microsoft Excel may organize and examine data. Excel is used by organizations for a wide variety of purposes, including budgeting, identifying trends, forecasting, and reporting.

How Can You Create a Business Budget in Excel?

Excel provides a selection of pre-made templates that may be used for either personal or business purposes. Establishing a business budget may be done in the fastest and least complicated way possible by using a budget spreadsheet adapted to your firm's specific requirements. These budgeting packages have input labels, analysis algorithms, and other spreadsheets with the most well-known budgeting variables, such as income, staff expenses, and operational expenditures. There is an option of creating your budget manually, in which case the user would be responsible for entering their labels, tables, and computations.

How Do You Track Business Expenses in Excel?

Excel provides users with a variety of templates they may use to keep an eye on their spending habits. One of the most common templates is called Expense Management, and it includes sections for a variety of different charges that are associated with running a company. Users can modify or delete column labels or headers so that the data meets their requirements more precisely. The format is intended to make it as easy as possible for the user to input data into the proper cells, and it has been designed to do just that. Users also have the option of manually compiling spending reports on their own.

1.2 History and Future of MS Excel

Excel has been available since 1982 under Multiplan, a widely used CP/M (Control Programs for Microcomputers) operating system. However, on MS-DOS systems, it was surpassed in popularity by Lotus 1-2-3. Microsoft released the Windows version of Excel v2.0 in 1987. In 1988, it began to outcompete Lotus 1-2-3 and the then-new QuatroPro, which had been released the previous year. The programming language Visual Basics for Applications, more often referred to as Macros, made its debut with Microsoft Excel version 5.0 for Windows in 1993. Because of this, the possibilities for automating processes, crunching numbers, and presenting data are almost limitless. Moreover, there are no limitations to the number crunching that may be done.

1.3 Present Day Microsoft Excel

Because it can be used to do almost any task associated with a business, Microsoft Excel has emerged as the industry standard and is now the most widely used business application in the world. There aren't many tasks that can't be finished with the assistance of Microsoft Office applications like Word, Outlook, and PowerPoint, amongst others.

Excel including other Office Suite provide an almost infinite number of customization options. As an example, the 10 built-in functions of Excel that are most often used and have the most impact are as follows:

- The capacity to construct models and conduct analyses on almost any form of data
- Concentrate as quickly as you can on the information that is most relevant to you.
- When creating graphs of data, use only one cell.
- You may access and use your spreadsheets from anywhere that has internet connectivity.
- People can do more when they work together.
- Make use of PivotCharts that are more active and interesting.
- Your data presentations need to have more of an attractive appearance aesthetically.
- Improve the speed and effectiveness with which you do tasks.
- Create spreadsheets that are both more complex and extensive with additional power.
- Publication and distribution of workbooks made possible with the use of Excel Services

Thanks to Visual Basic for Applications (VBA), an even greater premium should be placed on a robust BI (Business Intelligences) platform with easy personalization and automation capabilities thanks to Visual Basic for Applications (VBA).

Do you want to find solutions to your company issues with the help of Microsoft Excel? Put your trust in this manual. You have experience working with small to large businesses and in a wide array of fields. This chapter will help you in making the most of Microsoft Excel, regardless of the size of your company, whether it be a major corporation or a little business.

1.4 The Future of Excel

What are the next steps to take? It is only reasonable that the requirements of the many would be prioritized above the few. For many people, keeping up with the ever-evolving platform offerings from Microsoft has become a full-time job. Microsoft Excel will remain in the top spot regarding data analysis, data visualization, and business intelligence (BI) procedures.

Because of the simplicity with which data can be accessed and worked on in collaboration, cloud computing is gaining a growing following among commercial enterprises. Excel has a bright future, with multi-user access to large quantities of data allowing for increased productivity in reporting, analysis, and total work output in the years to come.

In the current highly competitive company environment, customized solutions are required to maintain a competitive edge over other industry companies and boost profits. Consultants specializing in Microsoft Excel are the most knowledgeable about the present and future of technology. To be valuable in the 21st century, it is essential to have a seasoned consulting business that can be contacted whenever necessary.

1.5 Data Functions, Formulas, and Shortcuts

Excel's "FUNCTION" feature refers to a predetermined formula that may be applied to certain data points in a sequence. A sum, count, maximum value, average, and lowest value may be found for a cell's range with a function, which can also be used for other simple jobs. For instance, the SUM function that calculates the total of a range A 1: A 2 may be found in the cell below, which is labeled A3.

- SUM is used to calculate the total of a set of numbers.
- A specified range of values may be used to calculate the AVERAGE using the term "AVERAGE."
- The COUNT function counts the number of things that fall inside a certain range.

The importance of the function

Excel users can do more tasks in little time, thanks to functions. Assume that you are interested in obtaining the overall sum for the allotted money for household items. You may do things simpler by using a formula to calculate the final sum. If you use the formula, you must refer to the cells E4 to E8 one at a time. You would need to use the formula that is shown below.

= E 4 + E 5 + E 6 + E 7 + E 8

If you were to use a function, you would express the formula in the question above as

=SUM (E 4: E 8)

It is far more effective to use the function to obtain the total of a variety of cells as opposed to using the formula, which will need to mention a lot of cells if you use it to get the sum, as you will see from the function that was used above to calculate the sum of a set of cells.

Common functions

Consider a good number of formula functions that are used most of the time in Microsoft Excel. You will begin with some fundamental functions in statistical analysis.

S/N	FUNCTION	CATEGORY	DESCRIPTION	USAGE
1	SUM	Math & Trig	Adds all the values in a range of cells	0
2	MIN	Statistical	Finds the minimum value in a range of cells	0
3	MAX	Statistical	Finds the maximum value in a range of cells	0
4	AVERAGE	Statistical	Calculates the average value in a range of cells	0
5	COUNT	Statistical	Counts the number of cells in a range of cells	0
6	LEN	Text	Returns the number of characters in a string text	3
7	SUMIF	Math & Trig	Adds all the values in a range of cells that meet a specified criteria. =SUMIF(range,criteria,[sum_range])	=SUMIF(D4:D8,">=1000",C4:C8)
08	AVERAGEIF	Statistical	Calculates the average value in a range of cells that meet the specified criteria. =AVERAGEIF(range,criteria,[average_range])	#DIV/0!
09	DAYS	Date & Time	Returns the number of days between two dates	#VALUE!
10	NOW	Date & Time	Returns the current system date and time	9/16/2022 15:53

Numeric Functions

These functions deal with numerical information, as one would expect from their name. The table that follows provides examples of various frequent arithmetic operations.

S/N	FUNCTION	CATEGORY	DESCRIPTION	USAGE
1	ISNUMBER	Information	Returns True if the supplied value is numeric and False if it is not numeric	TRUE
2	RAND	Math & Trig	Generates a random number between 0 and 1	0.862478391
3	ROUND	Math & Trig	Rounds off a decimal value to the specified number of decimal points	3.14
4	MEDIAN	Statistical	Returns the number in the middle of the set of given numbers	4
5	PI	Math & Trig	Returns the value of Math Function PI(π)	3.141592654
6	POWER	Math & Trig	Returns the result of a number raised to a power. POWER(number, power)	16
7	MOD	Math & Trig	Returns the Remainder when you divide two numbers	1
8	ROMAN	Math & Trig	Converts a number to roman numerals	MCMLXXXIV

String functions

Excel's built-in functions for manipulating text data include the ones listed below. The following table overviews some of the most frequent string functions.

S/N	FUNCTION	CATEGORY	DESCRIPTION	USAGE	COMMENT
1	LEFT	Text	Returns a number of specified characters from the start (left-hand side) of a string	#NAME?	Left 4 Characters of "GURU99"
2	RIGHT	Text	Returns a number of specified characters from the end (right-hand side) of a string	#NAME?	Right 2 Characters of "GURU99"
3	MID	Text	Retrieves a number of characters from the middle of a string from a specified start position and length. #NAME?	#NAME?	Retrieving Characters 2 to 5
4	ISTEXT	Information	Returns True if the supplied parameter is Text	FALSE	value – The value to check.
5	FIND	Text	Returns the starting position of a text string within another text string. This function is case-sensitive. =FIND(find_text, within_text, [start_num])	#NAME?	Find oo in "Roofing", Result is 2
6	REPLACE	Text	Replaces part of a string with another specified string. #NAME?	#NAME?	Replace "oo" with "xx"

Date Time Functions

Such functions are utilized to alter the date values sent to them. The following table presents examples of several of the most often date functions.

S/N	FUNCTION	CATEGORY	DESCRIPTION	USAGE
1	DATE	Date & Time	Returns the number that represents the date in excel code	2/4/2015
2	DAYS	Date & Time	Find the number of days between two dates	#VALUE!
3	MONTH	Date & Time	Returns the month from a date value	=MONTH("4/2/2015")
4	MINUTE	Date & Time	Returns the minutes from a time value	=MINUTE("12:31")
5	YEAR	Date & Time	Returns the year from a date value	=YEAR("04/02/2015")

Chapter 2: Why Learn Excel 2022?

In this chapter, you will go through why to learn Excel formulas and some of the basic Excel formulas in an excel spreadsheet.

2.1 Why Use Formulas?

This list is for you if you have ever questioned whether it is beneficial to spend time learning Excel formulae. Your expertise with formulas may aid you in various ways since they are the glue that holds spreadsheets together across the globe.
If you've ever considered whether it's worth your time to learn Excel formulae, this list can help you decide.

Because formulas are at the core of spreadsheets, becoming proficient in their use may benefit you in various contexts. Here are 10 motives why you should make it a priority to improve your familiarity with formulae, which you can read about below.

1. Formulas are essential for many different types of work. Over ninety percent of respondents regarding formulae said Excel formulas were "essential," "extremely important," or "critical" to the performance of their work duties.
2. Formulas are an effective tool for documenting and storing a solution that is currently in use (examples). They allow you to redo the answer anytime you choose and do it with pinpoint precision every time. They are a significant improvement over your poor memory.
3. Formulas are a useful tool for bringing your ideas into the actual world. Have you ever had the experience when you can describe what you need to achieve in simple English, but you've no clue how to accomplish it in Excel? You can construct the analysis that is in your thoughts using formulas.
4. Your familiarity with mathematical formulae enables you to create more effective spreadsheets. You can arrange data in a manner that makes use of formulae, which significantly decreases the number of mistakes and the amount of troubleshooting required. (To be honest, Pivot Tables also assist you in accomplishing the same goal.)
5. Since very few people are proficient with Excel formulae, having proficiency in this area is an opportunity to put oneself at a distance from the race by delivering more value and being more productive. And productivity is something that every company strives for.
6. If you are skilled with formulae, you will be able to construct beautiful solutions that do not involve a lot of intricacies. There is nothing in Excel that is more harmful than needless complexity since it makes it hard to comprehend whether a spreadsheet is truly running well or not.
7. Because choices in the corporate world are often made using spreadsheets, having a strong understanding of formulae allows you to be close to your action.
8. Formulas let you easily visualize facts. When you use formulae alongside conditional formatting, you can "see" significant patterns, insights, and correlations instantly.
9. If you're good with formulae, you'll have a whole set of razor-sharp tools at your disposal while trying to solve difficulties. Without formula expertise, you are compelled to employ a dull saw for every work, regardless of how lengthy or repetitive it may be.
10. Formulas allow you to go home on time. If you can complete your task more quickly and have more time to spend with your friends and family, you should learn how to apply formulae. Priceless.

2.2 How to Add Text to a Cell in Excel?

Once you have mastered the process of entering data into an Excel spreadsheet, creating data tables won't take as much time as before. If you haven't been told how to input data before, it may be a bit difficult; thus, you must stick to the guidelines below to discover the tips and tricks for simply entering your data into your spreadsheet.

Entering data in Excel worksheet

Cells in a worksheet may have either a value (such as a number or date) or a label (which can be either text or another cell's label). First, you'll need to move your cell pointer to the desired location before you can begin entering data. As you enter data, you'll see it on the worksheet (within the example below, text displays in cell A 1) and into your Formula Bar.

2. Enter the data into the field and press ENTER. When you click on a cell, the focus will shift to the next available cell below. You may prevent data from being typed into a cell by pressing ESC instead of entering.

Deleting & replacing data

To remove information from a cell, click on the cell and then hit the DELETE key.
Simply overwrite the contents of a cell with new text to replace it. The old information will be deleted when the new information is in place.

Using Undo & Redo

Sometimes, you may input information to realize that you messed it up.
Most of the time, you wish you could return to your position before committing the error. Don't worry if this occurs; click the "Undo" button to undo your most recent action.

You can keep pressing it until you reach a point where you once again feel like you are in control of the situation.
You also can click the "Redo" button if you make a mistake that causes you to go back more than one step. These buttons are amazing, and I see that you use them often.

Overlapping data

When you put data into a too wide column for the data you entered, it will spill over into the following column. The word "Travel Expenses" is placed into cell A1 in the example that can be seen below; nonetheless, it gives the impression that the content is contained in cell B1. When you choose cell A1 and look at the Formula bar, you can see that both letters are in that cell.

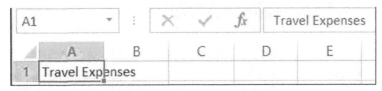

You are free to keep the content if you do not intend to use the column it is extending since it overlaps. However, as quickly as you insert text into the cell overlapped, it will seem as if your content has been lost. This effect will remain until you remove one of the overlapping cells. The phrase "Amount exclusive of GST" has been inserted into cell C3 of the example that can be seen below. However, a portion of the information in cell C3 is obscured by the contents of cell D3.

When cell C3 is selected, the Formula Bar updates to display the selected cell's contents. The width of column C must be modified so that the whole text of cell C 3 may be seen at once.

2.3 Excel Multiplication Formula

Since multiplying data is one of the operations used the most in Excel, the fact that there are multiple methods to do this task should not surprise anybody.

You are free to use whatever way while working with your spreadsheet on either a Mac or a PC will allow you to achieve the goals you have set for yourself.

The following are some of the most straightforward approaches to multiplying numbers:

Instructions for multiplying in Excel

This may be achieved quickly & easily by utilizing a simple formula to multiply values in a single cell.

If you enter "=2*6" into the cell and hit Enter, the cell should update to show the number 12.

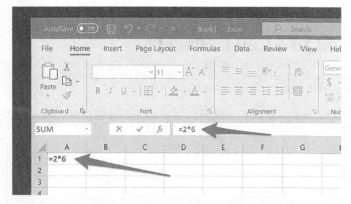

Utilizing the star as a multiplicator is the most straightforward method.

In addition, you may multiply the contents of two distinct cells together.

1. In one of the cells, enter "=."
2. Navigate to the cell that houses the first value you would like to multiply and click there.
3. Type "*".
4. Select the second cell you want to multiply by clicking on it.
5. Hit Enter.

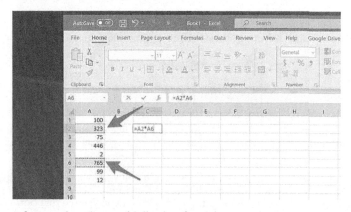

By clicking on the cells, you may reference them in a multiplication formula.

How to multiply numbers & cells using the PRODUCT formula

When utilizing the PRODUCT formula, you are not restricted to multiplying only two cells at once; rather, you may multiply anywhere from two to 255 values simultaneously.

You can multiply individual cells and integers using this formula by splitting them with commas, & you can multiply a sequence of cells using a colon.

For instance, the formula "= PRODUCT (A 1, A 3: A 5, B 1, 10)" instructs Excel to do the multiplication (A 1 x A 3 x A 4 x A 5 x B 1 x 10) since the A 3: A 5 instruction instructs Excel to perform the multiplication on A 3, A 4, and A 5.

Keep in mind that the order in which these cells & numbers are entered does not affect the multiplication result.

The formula for multiplying a column of numbers by a fixed number

Suppose you need to multiply a set of integers by the same factor. A direct reference to a cell containing the constant is all that's needed to do this.

The first step is to arrange the numbers to be multiplied into a column and then enter the constant into a separate cell.

Simply select the first cell to be multiplied, then write "=" in a new cell.

Input the name of a cell containing the constant, followed by a "$" before the letter and the number. The dollar sign makes this an exact reference, so you can copy & paste it into the spreadsheet without worrying about any changes.

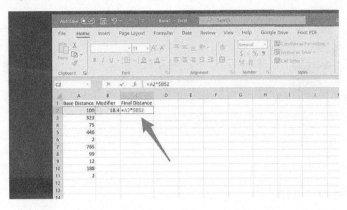

It's easy to refer to specific cells inside a formula using the $ symbol.

4. Hit Enter.

5. You may now execute the multiplication on either number by copying and pasting what you have just seen into other cells. Drag it by its bottom right corner to replicate a cell, as described in the previous sentence. This is the simplest method.

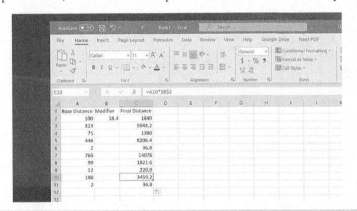

2.4 IF Function of Excel

The IF function is a check function that returns one value depending on whether a statement is true. However, it returns a different value depending on whether a statement is false. You can compare a value to your forecast throughout the functionality.

The following values may be sent into the IF function to be evaluated.

=IF (Logical_text, [Value_if_true], [Value_if_false])

- The value or logical expression that must be assessed and categorized as TRUE or FALSE is called "logical text" (Required Argument).
- (Probable Defense) Value if correct This value will be shown after the reasonable assessment if it is found to be TRUE.
- If the rational evaluation generates a FALSE result, the value of false (Possible Argument) will be returned.

To perform this function, the following logical operators may be utilized:

Equal to (=)

- Greater than (>)

Greater than or equal to (≥)

Less than (<)

Less than or equal to (≤)

Not equal (≠)

Check to verify that the number in the A2 cell is more than 500. =IF (Yes" and "No"; A2>500)

SEARCH =IF(A2>500,"Yes", "No")

	A	B	C	D	E	F	G
1	Price	Result					
2	400	=IF(A2>500,"Yes", "No")					
3	800	IF(logical_test, [value_if_true], [value_if_false])					
4	212						
5	454						
6	789						

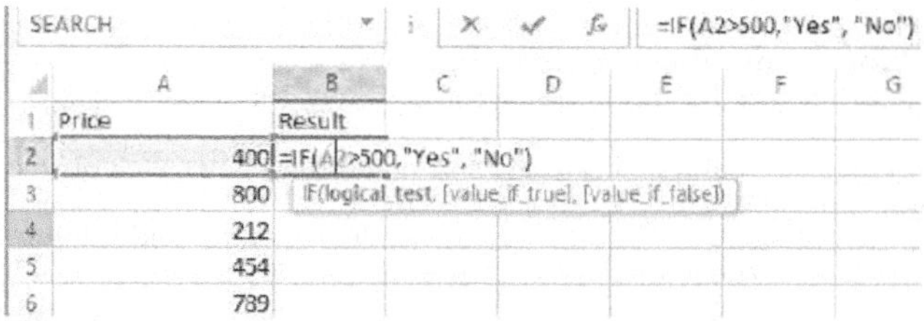

Stick to the steps in the preceding section to determine the values of A3 through B6: A3 must be more than 500, "Yes," "No," A4 must be greater than 500, "Yes," "No," A5 must be greater than 500, and A6 must be greater than 500, "Yes," "No."

C13

	A	B	C	D
1	Price	Result		
2	400	No		
3	800	Yes		
4	212	No		
5	454	No		
6	789	Yes		

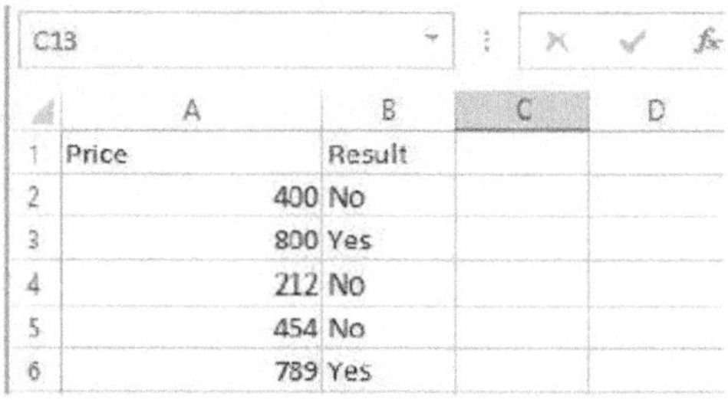

2.5 Excel Array Formula

You can conduct several computations all at once with the assistance of an array formula, or it can conduct one or more computations an unlimited number of times inside a certain cell range.
In these formulae, the referenced values might occur in the form of values inside a row, inside a column, or within a matrix (columns & rows). It is much simpler to present some instances to provide a more in-depth explanation of the array formula.

Without your Array Formula

You may see a variety of fruits listed in the illustration below (A2: A9), together with the quantity sold each day (B2: B9) & price per item (C2: C9). Within every revenue column cell, the revenue for each fruit is computed (D2: D9). Using a formula for multi-cell arrays will allow you to do this task more quickly.

D2 =B2*C2

	A	B	C	D
1	Product	Amount	Price	Revenue per fruit
2	Apple	236	€0,15	€35,40
3	Pear	178	€0,18	€32,04
4	Pineapple	55	€2,11	€116,05
5	Peach	98	€0,98	€96,04
6	Banana	215	€0,54	€116,10
7	Melon	102	€1,63	€166,26
8	Lemon	88	€1,15	€101,20
9	Kiwi	132	€0,86	€113,52
10	Total fruit revenue			€776,61

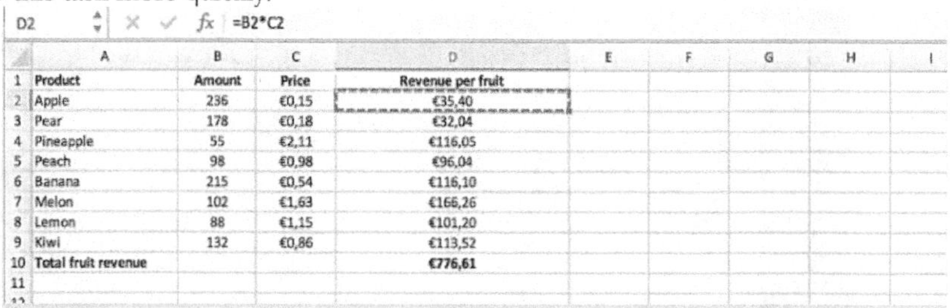

Multi Cells Array Formula

Using just one formula, the multi cells array formula would yield various outcomes that may be found anywhere inside a column or row. To calculate all the values of the column labeled "Revenue per fruit" at the same time in the example that was just shown, you begin by choosing the cell range inside which you wish to publish the results, and then you hit the F2 key to choose the first cell within range:

D2

	A	B	C	D
1	Product	Amount	Price	Revenue per fruit
2	Apple	236	€0,15	
3	Pear	178	€0,18	
4	Pineapple	55	€2,11	
5	Peach	98	€0,98	
6	Banana	215	€0,54	
7	Melon	102	€1,63	
8	Lemon	88	€1,15	
9	Kiwi	132	€0,86	
10	Total fruit revenue			

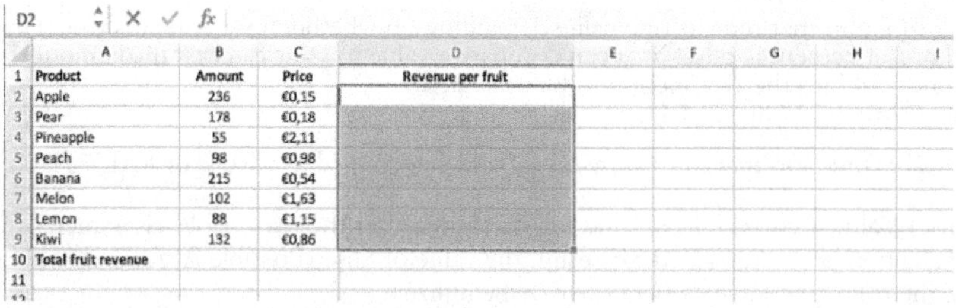

After that, you put the following formula into the chosen cell D2 of the array:

SUM =B2:B9*C2:C9

	A	B	C	D
1	Product	Amount	Price	Revenue per fruit
2	Apple	236	€0,15	=B2:B9*C2:C9
3	Pear	178	€0,18	
4	Pineapple	55	€2,11	
5	Peach	98	€0,98	
6	Banana	215	€0,54	
7	Melon	102	€1,63	
8	Lemon	88	€1,15	
9	Kiwi	132	€0,86	
10	Total fruit revenue			

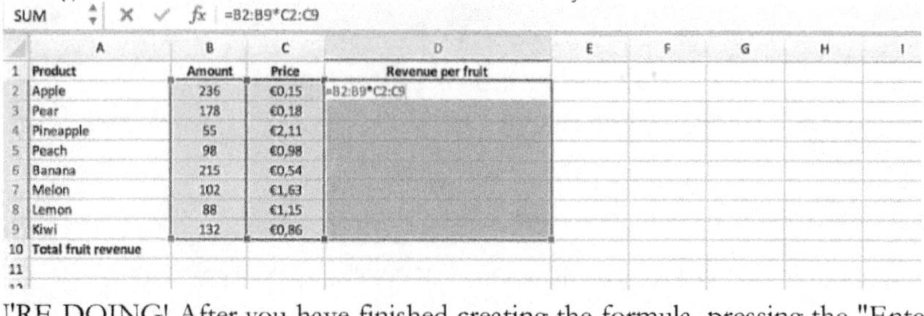

BUT STOP WHAT YOU'RE DOING! After you have finished creating the formula, pressing the "Enter" key will cause Excel to solely compute the outcome of the current row. This formula is identified as a CSE formula, and the reason for this is that it can only run properly when the keys CTRL, SHIFT, and ENTER are pressed simultaneously.

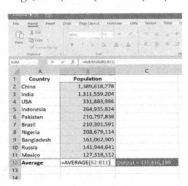

As can be seen, the formula computed all the array's values at the same time. Excel indicated that the calculation was an array function by adding brackets {} in the appropriate places around it.

Single Cell Array Formula

The formula for an individual cell array will only yield one result inside that cell, even though it may execute one or more computations. In this example, your total income from the fruit may, of course, be determined by using a SUM function to the numbers that are found in the column labeled "Revenue per fruit":

In contrast, while using your array function, you may skip through the intermediate sums without impacting the final tally. You choose the cell where you wish to share the sum of fruit sales and input the formula =SUM (B2: B9 * C2: C9):

To see the outcomes, use CTRL + SHIFT + ENTER once again. By just hitting Enter, you will trigger the '#VALUE!' error typical of Excel. After successfully running the array function, the sum will be shown in the corresponding cell, and brackets will once again surround the starting formula to indicate that it pertains to an array formula.

Functions that work with arrays may be risky.

Array functions are something that you see as potentially risky since they make collaboration inside a single spreadsheet very mistake prone. It's possible that your colleague is not acquainted with array methods and accidentally changed anything without using CTRL+SHIFT+ENTER.

2.6 Average Formulas in Excel

Using the AVERAGE function, you will understand the information well, such as the average number of owners in a certain shareholding pool.

=AVERAGE (number 1, [number 2], …)

Example:

=AVERAGE (B 2: B 11) – Shows the simple average, like (SUM (B 2: B 11)/10)

2.7 Percentage Formula in Excel

A figure expressed as a fraction of one hundred is referred to as a percentage. The notation for a percentage is a percent sign, which is written after a number. For instance, the notation for ten percent, sometimes known as 10%, is represented as 10/100. There are no units associated with the percentage.

Calculations were simplified thanks to the percentage that was provided. It may be tricky to precisely portray a part transgression, such as one-twelfth, two-thirds, etc., in written form. However, converting the fraction into a percentage is a simple process. As a result, the % is used in many aspects of your day-to-day lives.

For instance, the value of the fraction 2/5th expressed as a % is expressed as 2/5 multiplied by 100, which is 40%.

Percentage Formulas

Calculations may be made using an equation known as a formula. The computations conducted by humans are neither precise nor speedy. Excel's calculating process is quite comparable to that of a calculator. The following is a discussion of the percentage formulas:

Profit percentage = Sale price - actual price / actual price x 100

Or

Profit percentage = (Sale price / cost price- 1) x100

The distinction between the retail price and the cost price of a product is known as the "selling price," and it is the cost for which the item is sold to customers. The profit percentage is the amount of money made from selling your product.

Loss percentage = Actual price - sale price / Actual price x 100

Or

Profit percentage = (1 - Sale price / Actual price) x 100

When the selling price is lower than the cost price, this results in a loss for the business. It indicates that the seller sold the item at prices that were lower than the price at which they originally acquired the item.

To calculate the loss percentage, you may also apply the profit percentage method. The essential distinction is that it will be expressed in negative form.

Difference percentage = (B / A - 1) X 100

Where A & B refer to the goods for which the percentage of the difference between them must be determined.

Average percentage = Sum of all commodities / Number of the commodities x 100

The sum of each commodity's price, divided by the total number of prices, is how the average price is arrived at. In other contexts, you could refer to it as an average.

First, let's talk over some of Excel's most prevalent functions.

Data Sorting

Excel makes it quite simple for you to sort the data with only a few clicks.

Built-in formula

Excel has several formulae that can be accessed from the tool bar at the very top of the screen. In addition, you can calculate the formulae that are shown on a formula bar.

Filtering of the data and a variety of graphics in addition to that, it can filter data and display it using a variety of charts, including bar charts, pie charts, and so on.

Excel gives you several other options for how you may utilize the % formula, including the difference between two numbers, the total percentage, the percentage drop, the percentage rise, and many more of these options. You will go through all the relevant cases to have a deeper comprehension.

Let's begin by discussing how to open any Excel file on a computer if anybody here is unfamiliar with the process.

Percentage formula

Excel's tool bar has a % sign integrated into the program. It is often located in the middle of a toolbar, as illustrated in the following image:

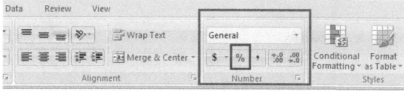

To turn a decimal number into a percentage, enter the decimal value into an Excel block, click on the block, and finally, click on the symbol for percentage (%) in the toolbar. The decimal figure that corresponds will have its equivalent percentage value translated for you.

Alternately, you may click the block that contains the decimal value and then hit the combination of Ctrl, Shift, & %. The decimal figure that corresponds will have its equivalent percentage value translated for you.

Examples depending on your percentage formula

Let's discuss several real-world applications of the % formula in Excel, covering various approaches.

Performing the calculations necessary to determine the percentages of 5 students across three disciplines.

The following is a breakdown of the performance of five students across three disciplines: Mathematics, English, and Science

Name	English	Mathematics	Science	Percentage
neha	76	79	82	
john	65	70	72	
Prince	62	75	69	
Swisha	82	90	88	
Tanu	54	62	72	

The following are the actions that need to be taken to compute the % of these three students:

The 1st thing you should to do is click on the first box in the % column, as seen in the following image:

Step 2: Position your cursor within the formula bar, then click, hold, and write "= (click on column number D, click on column number E, click upon this column number F)/300."
The formula for it will be written as "= (C: C + D: D + E: E)/300%." The names of the columns are automatically supplied as C: C, D: D, and E: E in this instance.
The data value will be automatically converted into the % whenever the percentage sign is used. The formula shown above may alternatively be written as:
The equation for calculating a percentage is as follows: "== (C: C + D: D + E: E) / 300 * 100."
(Total points divided by number of topics multiplied by 100)
It will be shown on a formula bar in the following format:

Press Enter. It will display the % value on the 1st block of a discount column.
After clicking once more on the 1st block in the % column, navigate your mouse to the block's lower-right corner and click there, as seen in the following image:

The next step is to move the point to a fifth box in the same column, which is labeled "Percentage," as illustrated in the following image:

The computation of the % value will take place on its own. Similarly, you may quickly determine the proportion of many pupils in a class with only a single click.

2.8 Excel Variance Formula

The dispersal of data points in a data collection from its mean is referred to as the "variance," It is calculated as the mean of the quadratic departure of every piece of data from the population mean. The word "variance" is often used interchangeably with "standard deviation." A formula for the variance may be calculated by first adding up the square deviation of every data point, then dividing the total by the complete number of the data points within a data set. This will give you the answer to the variance. In mathematical terms, this would look like this:

$\sigma^2 = \sum (X_i - \mu)^2 / N$

where,
X_i = ith data point within data sets
μ = Population means

N = Number of the data points within a population

Examples of the Variance Formula (Using Excel Template)

Let's look at an example of the Variance computation so you can have a better idea of how it works.

Variance Formula

Let's use the scenario of a class with five kids as an example. The students in the class each had a medical checkup, during which they were given their weight, and the relevant data was recorded: Determine the data set's standard deviation using the information that has been provided.

	A	B
4		
5	Students	Weight in Kg (X)
6	1	30
7	2	33
8	3	39
9	4	29
10	5	34
11		
12	N	5
13		

Solution:

The formula to determine the population means is as follows:

	A	B
4		
5	Students	Weight in Kg (X)
6	1	30
7	2	33
8	3	39
9	4	29
10	5	34
11		
12	N	5
13		
14	Population Mean is calculated as:	
15		
16	Formula	=SUM(B6:B10)/B12
17	Population Mean (μ)	33
18		

- Population Means = (30 kg + 33 kg + 39 kg + 29 kg + 34 kg) / 5
- Population Means = 33 kg

The next step is to compute the deviation, also known as the disparity between the individual data points & the average value.

C6   fx   =B6-B16

	A	B	C
4			
5	Students	Weight in Kg (X)	Deviation (X - μ)
6	1	30	-3
7	2	33	
8	3	39	
9	4	29	
10	5	34	
15			
16	Population Mean (μ)	33	
17			

In the same manner, compute each value included inside the data collection.

	A	B	C
4			
5	Students	Weight in Kg (X)	Deviation (X - μ)
6	1	30	-3
7	2	33	0
8	3	39	6
9	4	29	-4
10	5	34	1
15			
16	Population Mean (μ)	33	
17			

Using the formulas below, you can get squared deviations from every data point.

	A	B	C	D
4				
5	Students	Weight in Kg (X)	Deviation (X - μ)	Squared Deviation $(X – μ)^2$
6	1	30	-3	9
7	2	33	0	0
8	3	39	6	36
9	4	29	-4	16
10	5	34	1	1
15				

To determine variance, one uses the following formula.

$$\sigma 2 = \sum (Xi–μ)\, 2 \,/\, N$$

	A	B	C	D
4				
5	Students	Weight in Kg (X)	Deviation (X - μ)	Squared Deviation $(X – μ)^2$
6	1	30	-3	9
7	2	33	0	0
8	3	39	6	36
9	4	29	-4	16
10	5	34	1	1
11				
12	N	5		
17				
18	Variance is calculated using the formula given below			
19	$\sigma^2 = \sum (X_i - μ)^2 / N$			
20				
21	Variance Formula	=SUM(D6:D10)/B12		
22	Variance	12.4		
23				

$\sigma 2 = (9+ 0+ 36+ 16+ 1) / 5$
$\sigma 2 = 12.4$
This means that the data set has a variance of 12.4

Example #2
As an example, let's imagine a new corporation with a total staff of eight individuals. Each person's age in the group is listed. Compute the sample's standard deviation using the data you've supplied.

	A	B
3		
4	Person	Age in Years (X)
5	1	23
6	2	32
7	3	27
8	4	37
9	5	35
10	6	25
11	7	29
12	8	40
13		
14	N	8
15		

Solution:
Population Mean can be assessed like:

	A	B
3		
4	Person	Age in Years (X)
5	1	23
6	2	32
7	3	27
8	4	37
9	5	35
10	6	25
11	7	29
12	8	40
13		
14	N	8
15		
16	Population Mean is calculated as:	
17		
18	Formula	=SUM(B5:B12)/B14
19	Population Mean (μ)	31
20		

Population Mean = (twenty three years+ thirty two years+ twenty seven years+ thirty seven years+ thirty five years+ twenty five years+ twenty nine years+ fourty years) / 8
Population Mean = Thirty one year
Deciding the deviation, or the disparity between individual data points & the average is the next step.

C5	▼ : × ✓ *fx*	=B5-B18	

	A	B	C
3			
4	Person	Age in Years (X)	Deviation (X - μ)
5	1	23	-8
6	2	32	
7	3	27	
8	4	37	
9	5	35	
10	6	25	
11	7	29	
12	8	40	
17			
18	Population Mean (μ)	31	
19			

Similarly, conduct the calculation for each value in the data collection.

	A	B	C
3			
4	Person	Age in Years (X)	Deviation (X - μ)
5	1	23	-8
6	2	32	1
7	3	27	-4
8	4	37	6
9	5	35	4
10	6	25	-6
11	7	29	-2
12	8	40	9
17			
18	Population Mean (μ)	31	
19			

The following step is to determine the total squared deviations of every data point, as illustrated below.

	A	B	C	D
3				
4	Person	Age in Years (X)	Deviation (X - μ)	Squared Deviation (X - μ)^2
5	1	23	-8	64
6	2	32	1	1
7	3	27	-4	16
8	4	37	6	36
9	5	35	4	16
10	6	25	-6	36
11	7	29	-2	4
12	8	40	9	81
13				

The next formula is utilized to determine the value of the variance.

$\sigma2 = \sum (Xi-\mu)\,2\,/\,N$

	A	B	C	D
3				
4	Person	Age in Years (X)	Deviation (X - μ)	Squared Deviation (X - μ)^2
5	1	23	-8	64
6	2	32	1	1
7	3	27	-4	16
8	4	37	6	36
9	5	35	4	16
10	6	25	-6	36
11	7	29	-2	4
12	8	40	9	81
13				
14	N	8		
19				
20	Variance is calculated using the formula given below			
21	σ² = Σ (X$_i$ - μ)² / N			
22				
23	Variance Formula	=SUM(D5:D12)/B14		
24	Variance	31.75		
25				

$\sigma2 = (64 + 1 + 16 + 36 + 16 + 36 + 4 + 81)\,/\,8$

$\sigma2 = 31.75$

Therefore, 31.75 is the value that represents the set's variance.

Explanation

Following are the steps that need to be taken to get a formula for the variance:

Create a population that is made up of many data points as the first step. Xi will denote these points of data.

Calculate the total number of information points within a population, which is indicated by the letter N. Step 2:

Calculating the population mean is the next step, which is accomplished by first adding every single data point & then dividing the sum by the total number of data points (which was determined in step 2) with in population. The symbol represents the average of the population.

$\mu = X5 + X4 + X3 + X2 + X1\,/\,N$

or

$\mu = \sum Xi/N$

As a fourth step, you may calculate the distance each data point is from the population mean by deducting the mean from every data point in the population; for example, you can write a deviation for the initial data point as (X 1 -), the second as (X 2 -), and so on.

Find your square root of all computed deviations from the mean in Step 4.

Following this, step 6 involves adding up the squared deviations from the mean that were determined, i.e. (X 1 -)2 + (X 2 -)2 + (X 3 -)2 +...... + (X n -)2 or (Xi -)2.

Seventh, divide the sum of squared deviations by the whole number of information points in the population from step 2, and you'll get the formula for a variance.

σ2 = ∑ (Xi–μ) 2 / N

Relevance & Uses of the Variance Formula

Because of its frequent use in probability distribution as a measure of a data set's dispersion (volatility) relative to its mean, variance is a crucial subject for statisticians to grasp. An investor's portfolio risk may be evaluated with the aid of the variance since volatility is a measure of risk. If the variance of a data collection is 0, then all the variables are the same. Conversely, a large variance may suggest that every data point differs from the mean. While a smaller variation indicates the contrary, a higher variance does not always indicate better reliability. Note that variance is always positive.

Chapter 3: Basic Excel Formulas

In this chapter, you will go through some basic ways to add up data in excel sheet, basic Excel formulas and Excel shortcuts in an excel spreadsheet.

3.1 Five Time-Saving Ways to Insert Data into Excel

When assessing your data using Excel, you may input basic formulas using one of five conventional techniques. The merits and cons of each strategy are distinct. Therefore, before you get into the main equations, you will go over those ways so that you may create your strategy.

1. Simple insertions: Typing your formula inside your cell

Excel's formulas, even the most fundamental ones, may be inserted by entering the formula directly into a cell or even the formula bar. Typically, this would start with an equal sign and the name of an Excel function.

Excel provides a function suggestion in the form of a pop-up window whenever you begin typing the name of a function into the program. You will have the ability to choose the solution that best suits your needs from this list. There is no need to use the Enter key. You may also continue adding options by using the Tab key. This is an alternative. In such a case, you could have an issue with the right name, which your browser will indicate with the question mark '#NAME?' Select the cell in question once again, and then under the formula bar, enter in the function you want to use to fix it so that it works correctly.

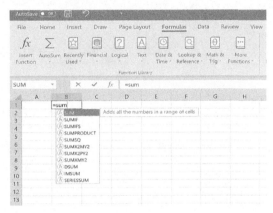

2. Using the Insert Function from your Formulas Tab

Using the Insert Function dialogue box in Excel is all that is required to insert functions into an Excel spreadsheet. You may do this by going to the Formulas tab and then choosing the Insert Function option from the drop-down menu. To complete your financial analysis, you may make advantage of the functions provided by the dialogue box.

3. Selecting your Formula from the Groups in your Formula Tab

You should use this option to get straight into your favorite features. To access this menu, choose the Formulas tab and select the group that best suits your needs. Simply clicking will bring up a sub-menu with a rundown of the available options. After you've settled on a decision, you'll be able to go on to the next step. If the group you want to use isn't mentioned there, go under the More Functions option; it may be hidden there.

4. Using AutoSum Option

The AutoSum tool is your best option for regular tasks. Therefore, go to the home tab in the upper right corner of the screen, and choose the AutoSum option. The other formulas that have been hidden will become visible after you click the caret. This option may also be found on the formulae tab beneath the option to Insert a Function.

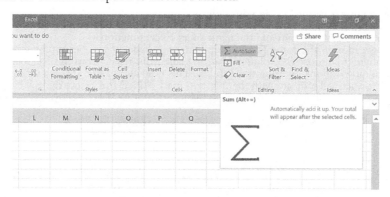

5. Quick Insert: Utilize Newly Used Tab

If you choose the option labeled Recently Used, you won't have to retype your most current formula as much as you would otherwise have to. "Formulas" is the third option on the menu next to "AutoSum" on the tab labeled "Formulas."

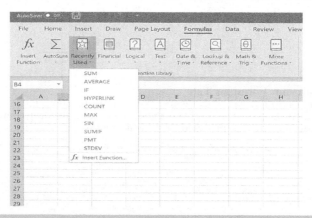

3.2 Basic Formulas for Excel Workflow

Since you are now able to accurately input and utilize your preferred formulae, let's have a look at some fundamental Excel functions so that you can get started.

4. COUNTA

The COUNTA program can count all cells in a range together with its COUNT function. However, it does count all cells, regardless of the kind of cell that they are. In contrast to COUNT, which only stores numerical information, it often counts the text, dates, days, sequences, logical values, and errors in addition to void strings and empty strings.

=COUNTA (VALUE 1, [VALUE 2], …)

Example:

COUNTA (C 2: C 13) – No matter how sorted the C column is, rows 2-13 will be tallied in that column. On the other hand, in contrast to COUNT, a comparable method cannot be used to count rows. You will need to modify the range between the brackets; for example, COUNTA (C 2: H 2) will count columns from C up to H.

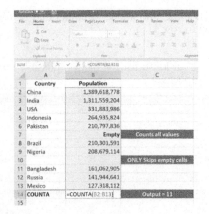

5. IF

This function may also be utilized if you choose the option to sort the data following a predetermined set of guidelines. The fact that you can use other formulae and functions is one of the many benefits of the IF formula.

=IF (LOGICAL TEST, [VALUE_IF_FALSE] [VALUE_IF_TRUE],)

Example:

=IF (C 2<D 3, 'TRUE,' 'FALSE') – It determines if the value at C 3 is less than the value at D 3 by comparing the two. If your logic is valid, let your cell value stay TRUE, or else FALSE

=IF (SUM (C 1: C 10)➔SUM (D 1: D 10), SUM (C 1: C 10), SUM (D 1: D 10)) – A challenging use of the IF logic. After initially totaling C 1 through C 10 and D 1 through D 10, it compares the results. A cell value becomes comparable to a sum of C 1-C10 when the quantity of C1-C10 present is more than the sum of D 1-D10 present in the cell. If not, it will be the whole amount from C1 through C10.

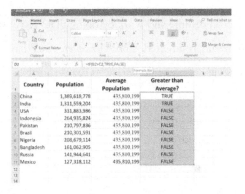

6. The TRIM

Using a TRIM function will guarantee that errant spaces do not bring about mistakes in your routines. It indicates that there are no free spots available. TRIM can only operate on a single cell, unlike many other works that can operate on various cells simultaneously. Because of this, it has the disadvantage of producing duplicate information inside a spreadsheet.

= TRIM (TEXT)

For Example:

TRIM (A 2) – Eliminates empty spaces from the values included in the A 2 cell.

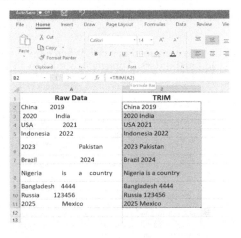

7. MAX & MIN

These MAX & MIN functions assist in discovering the values that are the highest and lowest possible inside a given collection of data.

=MIN (NUMBER 1, [number 2], …)

Example:

=MIN (B 2: C 11) – In each of the columns, B and C, the smallest number may be found in the B column beginning at row 2 and in the C column beginning at row 2 and going up to row 11.

=MAX (NUMBER 1, [number 2], …)

Example:

=MAX (B 2: C 11) – In both columns, B and C, it looks for the highest possible number in the B column between rows 2 and 11 and in the C column between rows 2 and 11, respectively.

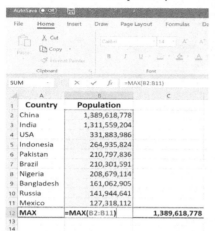

3.3 Excel Shortcuts

Excel keyboard shortcuts let you work more quickly and efficiently. The toolbar may be accessed with 2 or 3 keystrokes rather than a mouse, which saves time. Don't you save a ton of time and work by doing that? Excel shortcuts accelerate the procedure, reducing the time needed to finish a job.

The answer to whether mastering these shortcuts is required is no. However, you'll have an advantage if you remember a few. After a lot of practice, you'll be able to remember the majority of the fundamental Excel shortcuts.

Let's review the top 50 Excel shortcuts that every user should know. 50 Excel shortcuts have been divided into groups based on their intended application. We'll start by looking at the worksheet's shortcut keys.

Workbook Shortcut Keys

Using a workbook is simple once you understand the basics. You'll discover how to create a new workbook, load any other workbook, and save a spreadsheet. After that, you'll look at utilizing the tab key to navigate between different worksheet pages.

Description	Excel Shortcuts
1. To create a new workbook	Ctrl + N
2. To open an existing workbook	Ctrl + O
3. To save a workbook/spreadsheet	Ctrl + S
4. To close the current workbook	Ctrl + W
5. To close Excel	Ctrl + F4
6. To move to the next sheet	Ctrl + PageDown
7. To move to the previous sheet	Ctrl + PageUp
8. To go to the Data tab	Alt + A
9. To go to the View tab	Alt + W
10. To go the Formula tab	Alt + M

Now that you've discovered some helpful Excel shortcuts put your spreadsheet out of your mind. The next step after creating a workbook is to format the cells.

Cell Formatting Shortcut Keys

All the data you're dealing with right now in Excel is contained in a cell. When editing cells, you may use several conveniences, such as aligning the contents of the cells and adding borders. Applying a border to all chosen cells is another option. The following list of Excel keyboard shortcuts is provided.

Description	Excel Shortcuts
11. To edit a cell	F2
12. To copy and paste cells	Ctrl + C, Ctrl + V
13. To italicize and make the font bold	Ctrl + I, Ctrl + B
14. To center align cell contents	Alt + H + A + C
15. To fill color	Alt + H + H
16. To add a border	Alt + H + B
17. To remove outline border	Ctrl + Shift + _
18. To add an outline to the select cells	Ctrl + Shift + &
19. To move to the next cell	Tab
20. To move to the previous cell	Shift + Tab
21. To select all the cells on the right	Ctrl + Shift + Right arrow
22. To select all the cells on the left	Ctrl + Shift + Left Arrow
23. To select the column from the selected cell to the end of the table	Ctrl + Shift + Down Arrow
24. To select all the cells above the selected cell	Ctrl + Shift + Up Arrow
25. To select all the cells below the selected cell	Ctrl + Shift + Down Arrow

Let's look at a few more advanced Excel shortcuts for formatting cells and the ones we've previously covered.
In this session, you will discover how to create a cell remark. Comments may help describe a cell's content in greater detail. You would be able to identify a value and then swap it out for another using the spreadsheet. Let's start with the basics: how to enter the current time and date, enable a filter, and add an interactive hyperlink to a single cell. The final format will be that of the data contained inside a cell.

Description	Excel Shortcuts
26. To add a comment to a cell	Shift + F2
27. To delete a cell comment	Shift + F10 + D
28. To display find and replace	Ctrl + H
29. To activate the filter	Ctrl + Shift + L Alt + Down Arrow
30. To insert the current date	Ctrl + ;
31. To insert current time	Ctrl + Shift + :
32. To insert a hyperlink	Ctrl + k
33. To apply the currency format	Ctrl + Shift + $
34. To apply the percent format	Ctrl + Shift + %
35. To go to the "Tell me what you want to do" box	Alt + Q

The next stage is to learn how to work with an entire row or column in Excel after dealing with the cell formatting shortcuts in the application.

Row and Column Formatting Shortcut Keys

Several significant shortcuts for formatting rows and columns will be taught to you.
In this chapter, you will learn how to hide and then re-show the selected columns and rows and delete whole rows and columns.

Description	Excel Shortcuts
36. To select the entire row	Shift + Space
37. To select the entire column	Ctrl + Space
38. To delete a column	Alt+H+D+C
39. To delete a row	Shift + Space, Ctrl + -
40. To hide selected row	Ctrl + 9
41. To unhide selected row	Ctrl + Shift + 9
42. To hide a selected column	Ctrl + 0
43. To unhide a selected column	Ctrl + Shift + 0
44. To group rows or columns	Alt + Shift + Right arrow
45. To ungroup rows or columns	Alt + Shift + Left arrow

After learning about the numerous shortcuts for formatting cells, rows, and columns in Microsoft Excel, you're prepared to move on to more complicated ideas, such as pivot tables. You may use the pivot table to summarize your data in several ways.

Pivot Table Shortcut Keys

Create a pivot table first using the sales data.
Under each product category, a pivot table summarizing overall sales with each product subcategory is available for viewing.

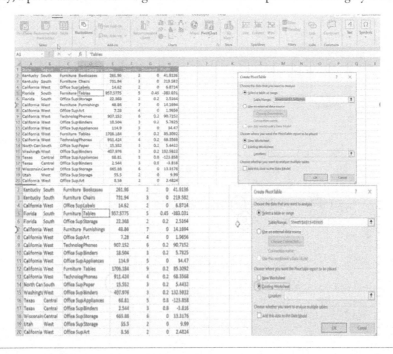

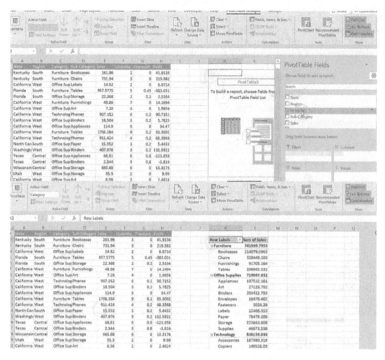

| 46. To group pivot table items | Alt + Shift + Right arrow |

The graph below shows that sales of chairs and bookcases fall within Group 1.

| 47. To ungroup pivot table items | Alt + Shift + Left arrow |
| 48. To hide pivot table items | Ctrl + - |

You'll see that you've hidden the subcategories for Chairs, Art, and Labels on this page.

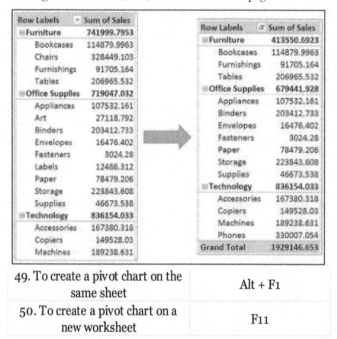

| 49. To create a pivot chart on the same sheet | Alt + F1 |
| 50. To create a pivot chart on a new worksheet | F11 |

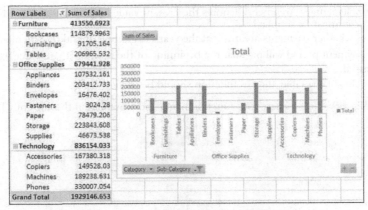

The creation of reports and analysis might be sped using Excel shortcut keys. After reading this guide, you should know several Excel shortcuts related to workbooks, cell formatting, row & column formatting, and pivot tables.

Chapter 4: Ten Advanced Excel Formulas

In this chapter, you will go through ten most advanced Excel formulas and Excel Formula cheat sheet.

4.1 Advanced Formulas

Some of the advanced Excel formulas are given below in detail.

1. PV Function

The PV equation, often known as the "Present Value" equation, calculates the present value of an obligation or investment by using a fixed interest rate together with the debt or investment. The PV function may be used for mortgages and other investments that have reoccurring, periodic fees; alternatively, a projected value (investment aim) equals PV can be employed instead (rate, nper, pmt, [fv], [type])

	A	B	C
1			
2	Annual Interest Rate	3.50%	
3	Periodic Payment	500	
4	Number of Periods (Monthly)	72	
5	Compounding Periods per year	12	
6	Present Value		
7			
8			
9			

Find out the table's current value by using the PV function.
In a blank cell, write the objective and the defense. PV = (B 2 / B 5, B 4, B 3, 0, 0)

SUM | ✓ | fx =PV(B2/B5, B4, B3,0,0)

	A	B	C	D
1				
2	Annual Interest Rate	3.50%		
3	Periodic Payment	500		
4	Number of Periods (Monthly)	72		
5	Compounding Periods per year			
6	Present Value	=PV(B2/B5, B4, B3,0,0)		
7		PV(rate, nper, pmt, [fv], [type])		

As can be seen in the following table, the total amount will change to a negative value of -£32,428.79 when you hit the enter key.

2. FV Function

The FV equation calculates the potential value of an investment or loan with a stable interest rate and a consistent dividend that is paid periodically.
The following conditions are necessary for the operation of the FV function.
=FV (rate, nper, pmt, [pv], [type])

- This is the interest rate that pertains to each period of compounding (necessary argument).
- This is the total amount of money a person will spend over their whole lifespan.
- The Pmt includes the payment date in its information (Supplementary Argument). The PV defense must be presented if this argument is not used.

- The acronym PV (Supplementary Argument) denotes the present value of the investment or loan. If the PV argument is not given, the Pmt parameter must be supplied.
- This variable indicates whether payments are made at the year's beginning or end (Supplementary Argument).
- If you input a 1, the payment period will begin at the beginning of the month. If you enter 0, the payment period will begin after the term has passed.

For determining the possible value of the table, the FV function should be used.

- B3/B5, B4*B5, 0, -B2, =FV Please insert your function name and argument in the currently blank area.

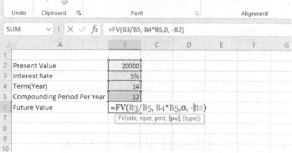

3. NPV Function

To assess the net current value of an investment, a computation known as an NPV function applies a discount rate to several prospective cash flows before concluding.
The following types of data may be fed into an NPV calculation.
(rate, value 1, [value 2]) = NPV
This is a representation of the rate of the lifetime discount (necessary argument).
It is the first payment or source of income in a string of transactions. Value 1: (Mandatory Argument) Outgoing transactions are represented by negative payments, whereas receiving payments are represented by positive payments. Value 1 is mandatory.
Its value reflects a diverse assortment of payments and income sources. Value2 (Optional Argument): This value is used to determine the investment's net present value.

- In a blank cell, write the objective and the defense.

SLN Function

The SLN function assists in the computation of the asset's depreciation throughout a single period by using a technique for straight-line deterioration.
The SLN function relies on the following inputs to fulfill its responsibilities.
=SLN (cost, salvage, life)
This is the first investment that must be made on an object that has been salvaged (obligatory argument).
This is the worth of the asset after it has reached the end of its useful life; it is also referred to as the item's salvage value at times. (Argument Taken for Granted)
Life is the total number of times an asset is written off, often referred to as the object's useful life.
In the next section, depreciation will be taken into consideration.

- In a currently empty cell, write the name of the function and a parameter.

= SLN (B 3, B 4, B 5)

4. SYD Function

A simplified yield determination, or SYD, is a method that may be used to calculate the number of years that an asset will depreciate over a certain period. This function considers the asset's cost, salvage value, and the number of times it has been depreciated.
The following are the inputs that may be given to a SYD function so it can conduct its tasks.
=SYD (cost, salvage, life, per)
This represented the asset's price when it was first purchased (obligatory argument).
Salvage (Required Argument) This is the asset's value after it has been depleted, also known as its salvage value.
(Obligatory Argument Regarding Life): The total amount of an asset's depreciation that takes place throughout its useful life.
The depreciation cost would be determined by considering the time (Required Argument).
The following table may be used to compute the total depreciation of the assets by adding up the years of depreciation shown in the table.

- In the empty box, you should provide the aim and the evidence that supports it.

= SYD (B 2, B 3, B 4, B 5)

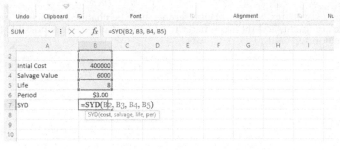

5. TEXTJOIN Function

The TEXTJOIN function combines the data from many cells or ranges by dividing each value with a delimiter and then applying the function. The Microsoft Excel 2022 that I have does not include this function. The following is a rundown of the processes involved in the TEXTJOIN function.
Delimiter, disregard empty, text1, [text2], =TEXTJOIN, and so forth.
Applying the TEXTJOIN FUNCTION allowed the texts in the table to be connected.
Choose the sort of empty cell you have and make the =TEXTJOIN parameter selection in the function (",", TRUE, A 2, A 3, A 4, A 5, A 6)
When you press the enter key, the texts will be combined into a single text string containing all the content you entered.

6. PROPER Function

Using the PROPER function, the cast of characters or text may be inverted. The words that come before the capital letter are written lower case in each text series.
The PROPER function calls for the submission of only one argument at a time. Use the =PROPER operator to change the case of text strings (Text)

- Enter the reason for your argument and your defense into the respective boxes. =PROPER(A2)

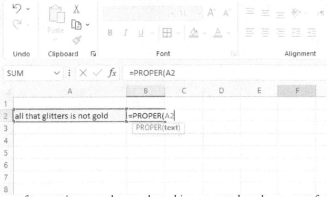

When you hit the enter key, the case of text strings you have selected is converted to the correct form, as illustrated below.

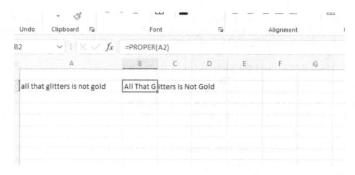

7. LOWER Function

By using the LOWER feature, an existing text string or cell reference may be changed to include just lowercase text characters. This function will only take one argument, and that parameter is =LOWER (Text). It is possible to transform the characters in the table to lowercase using the function LOWER.

To make the following modifications to text strings, use the LOWER feature:

- Place both the goal and the defense in the blank cell labeled "LOWER" (A2).

The text strings in the table below will be converted to lower case when you hit enter on your keyboard.

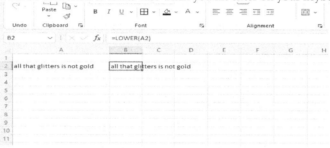

8. IFFEROR Function

The IFFEROR function generates a one-of-a-kind response if a formula produces an incorrect result. In place of several nested IF statements, the IFERROR logs and manages error information.

The IFERROR operates with these various settings for its parameters.

(Value, value if error) =IFFERROR Value (required argument). It may refer to either a thought or a statement that has been investigated or for which flaws have been identified.

The value may be returned even if there is an error in the formula (Required Argument).

Let's use the IFFEROR function to create a specialized message that reads "invalid data" rather than the faults shown in the table below.

Follow the procedures mentioned below to correct the problem in cell C2.

- In a currently empty cell, write the name of the function and the parameters it accepts.

A2/B2, "invalid data," =IFERROR

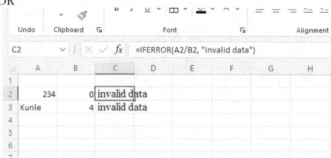

9. AND Function

The AND function checks to see whether the criteria specified in a data set are true and returns a result of FALSE if any of the requirements are not met. For example, B1 is more than 50, but less than 100 is a condition that would provide a FALSE result.

The following arguments are passed into the AND function when it is invoked.

(logical1, [logical2],) = AND 1 rational (Necessary Argument) The logical2 standard is the first logical quality that must be analyzed and defined (Optional Argument). The second stage of the evaluation process is known as the logical value.

To get the results of the table, as was previously mentioned.

- In a currently empty cell, please write the name of the function and the parameters it accepts.
A2 > 67, A2 > A3

=AND(A2>67,A2<A3)

	A	B	C	D
1				
2	23	FALSE		
3	56			
4				

The result of the AND function in the table is FALSE because one of the constraints in the data set, namely, that A2 is not bigger than 67, was not met.
The following table demonstrates that the AND feature will return the value TRUE when all the prerequisites for the dataset have been met.

=AND(A2>20,A2<A3)

	A	B	C	D
1				
2	23	TRUE		
3	56			
4				

10. OR Function

The OR function will return the value TRUE if all the conditions are satisfied; otherwise, it will return the value FALSE. In contrast to the AND function, the result will be interpreted as false if any criteria are not satisfied.
The OR function takes the following arguments, which are referred to as parameters:
First Logic, then Second Logic The first criterion that must be satisfied or logical value must be determined is = OR logical1 (Required Argument).
(Important counterargument) Logical: The second essential step is demonstrating that the line of reasoning is sound.
To get the results that are shown in the table above.
=OR(A2>30, B2>50, B3=45) In the space provided, type in the function's name and the input arguments.

As you can find in the subsequent paragraph, the response will be FALSE when you click enter.

4.2 Excel Formulas: The Cheat Sheet

Date and Time Formula	
=NOW	Put up the current time and date
=TODAY()	Simply display today's date without time.
=DAY(TODAY())	Display the current date in a cell.
=MONTH(TODAY())	Format a cell to display the current month.
=TODAY()+10	Increase the current date by 10 days.
Rounding and Counting Formulas	
=SUM	Adds up a set of numbers
=AVERAGE	Finds the average of certain values.
=COUNT	Determines how many cells within a given range contain a numerical value.
=INT	decimal places from a number
=ROUND	Provides the ability to choose the precision with which a number is rounded.
=IF	Checks to see whether a situation is real or imagined
=SUMIF	Performs a sum calculation using a set of variables for which a criterion has been satisfied.

=COUNTIF	Determines the number of cells inside a given range that meet the specified criteria and counts them.
=COUNTA(A1:A5)	Count the number of cells that are not blank in each range.
=ROUND(1.45, 1)	1.45 is rounded to the next decimal point.
=ROUND(-1.457, 2)	-1.457 is rounded to 2 decimal places here.
=TRUE	This function will return a logical number. TRUE
=FALSE	This function will return a logical number. FALSE
=AND	If each of its parameters is true, this function will return TRUE.
=OR	Gives a value of TRUE if any of the arguments are true.
Unit Conversion Formulas	
=CONVERT(A1,"day","hr")	Performs the conversion from the value of A1 in days to hours.
=CONVERT(A1,"hr","mn")	This function takes the value of A1 and converts it from hours to minutes.
=CONVERT(A1,"yr", "day")	Performs a year-to-days conversion on the value of A1.
=CONVERT(A1,"C","F")	Performs a temperature conversion from Centigrade to Fahrenheit for the value of A1.
=CONVERT(A1,"tsp","tbs")	Adjusts the value of A1 such that it is in tablespoons rather than teaspoons.
=CONVERT(A1,"gal","l")	Performs the conversion from gallons to liters for the value of A1.
=CONVERT(A1,"mi","km")	The value of A1 is expressed in kilometers, converted from miles
=CONVERT(A1,"km","mi")	Calculates the value of A1 in terms of miles and kilometers.
=CONVERT(A1,"in","ft")	A1's value is converted from inch to feet and vice versa.
=CONVERT(A1,"cm","in")	This function provides a conversion from centimeters to inches for the value of A1.
=BIN2DEC(1100100)	1100100 is converted to decimal form via this function (100)
=ROMAN	Performs the conversion of a number to its Roman numeral equivalent.
Mathematics	
=B2-C9	Finds the difference between the values within two cells
=D8*A3	Perform a multiplication using the numbers found in the two cells.
=PRODUCT(A1:A19)	increases the number of cells that fall inside the range.
=PRODUCT(F6:A1,2)	multiply the cells that fall inside the range, and then multiply the resulting number by 2.
=A1/A3	Performs a division by the number in A1 using the value in A3.
=MOD	After the division has been completed, this function gives the remainder.
=MIN(A1:A8)	Determines the lowest possible value inside a given range.
=MAX(C27:C34)	Determines the highest possible value inside a given range.
=SMALL(B1:B7, 2)	Determines the number that is the second smallest inside a range.
=LARGE(G13:D7,3)	Determines the number that is the third biggest in each range.
=POWER(9,2)	Determine the square of nine
=9^3	Works out the cube of nine
=FACT(A1)	A1's value factorization
=EVEN	It raises numbers to the closest even number.
=ODD	Increases or decreases a number to the next even or odd number.
=AVERAGE	Determines the mean
=MEDIAN	Finding the middle number
=SQRT	Determines the square root of the given number
=PI	Pi value is displayed.
=POWER	Produces the answer to a power calculation
=RAND	The function returns a random integer between 0 & 1.
=RANDBETWEEN	It gives back a random number within the range you provide.
=COS	Finds a cosine of the given number
=SIN Function that gives back the sine of an input angle	returns the exact sine of a specified angle
=TAN	Provides an accurate tangent calculation
=CORREL	The method determines the degree of association between two datasets
=STDEVA	Calculates a sample's standard deviation estimate
=PROB	Provides the likelihood that a set of values falls inside a certain interval
Text Formulas	
=LEFT	Takes a character or characters from the beginning of a string of text.
=RIGHT	Pulls a character or characters from the end of a string of text.
=MID	Takes out the middle characters of a string of text.
=CONCATENATE	Combines several text strings into one
=REPLACE	Deletes and replaces specified characters in a string of text
=LOWER	Turns a string of text into lowercase.
=UPPER	Changes the case of a string of text.
=PROPER	Fixes the capitalization of a text string.
=LEN	Gives back the quantity of characters into your text string.
=REPT	Iterates a certain amount of text again and over
=TEXT	Converts a numerical value to text format.
=VALUE	Changes the value of a cell from text to numeric format.
=EXACT	Compares the contents of two text values to check whether they are the same.
=DOLLAR	Makes a digit string using the US Dollar currency format.
=CLEAN	Cleans text of all non-printable characters.
Finance	
=INTRATE	Interest on a fully invested investment may be computed.
=EFFECT	Determines the true yearly percentage rate
=FV	Determines how much money investment will be worth in the future.

=FVSCHEDULE	Determines how much a sum of money will be worth in the future based on a compound interest rate schedule.
=PMT	Determines the whole cost of a debt security (principal plus interest).
=IPMT	Provides a method for determining the amount of interest to be paid on financial investment within a specified period
=ACCRINT	Computes the interest accumulated on a security with a periodic interest payment schedule.
=ACCRINTM	Accumulates interest until the maturity date of security which pays interest.
=AMORLINC	The depreciation is computed for every accounting period.
=NPV	Establishes how much income will be made in the upcoming after subtracting the discount rate from future cash flows.
=YIELD	Yield is determined by the security's maturity, par value, and interest rate.
=PRICE	Useful for determining the cost of a $100 full bond price with a variable coupon rate.

Chapter 5: Modifying the Worksheet

Worksheet cells may need insertion, relocation, or deletion throughout normal editing. Existing cells and their contents change to accommodate for the alterations made to neighboring cells when cells are modified and transferred.

5.1 Moving to a Specific Cell

Let's look at how to relocate cells in a spreadsheet now.

- Choose the cell(s) you want to relocate.
- To modify the chosen cells, roll the mouse over their borders.
- To reposition the cells, just click and drag them.

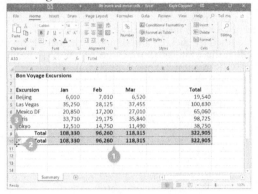

Moreover, all cells are relocated.

5.2 Adding a Row & Column

Simply choose a cell in the column and use Home ➔ Insert ➔ Insert the Sheet Columns or Remove Sheet Columns to make changes. Alternately, you may right-click the column header and choose Insert or Delete from the context menu that appears.

Insert / delete the row

You may insert or delete rows from a worksheet by selecting a cell in the row and clicking Home ➔ Insert ➔ Insert the Sheet Rows. Otherwise, you may right-click a row's number and choose either Delete or Insert from the context menu.

Formatting options

Selecting a formatted row or column allows you to copy the formatting to a newly inserted column or row. After inserting, pick the Insert Alternatives button and then one of the following options if you do not wish your data formatting to be employed:

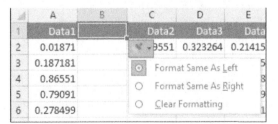

Suppose you don't see the Insert Settings icon. In that case, you may enable it by selecting File ➔ Options ➔ Advanced, then select the Show Insert Settings buttons option under the Cut, copy, & paste section.

5.3 Shortcut Menu

When you hit the Right button on your mouse, you'll see a selection of shortcut menus.
You may also simultaneously bring up the shortcut menu by pressing the (Shift) key and the F10 key.
A shortcut menu may be activated anywhere, and more than fifty menus are already predefined.
A shortcut menu that appears if you have one cell selected may be accessed via the menu that can be found below.

After making your selection in the cell labeled "B2," click the mouse's right button. The following menu of quick-access items will then be shown.

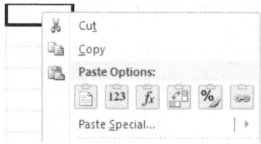

Note that the shortcut menu is shown below where the mouse is now positioned.
A shortcut menu does not include all the commands available to your disposal in its list of options. There are situations when it will not show you the command for which you are searching.

5.4 Resizing a Column and Row

Simply choose the columns you want to modify the width of, and then enter the new width in the text box that appears.
Position the cursor among the column titles to the right of the column or columns of interest.
When the mouse is in the right spot, it becomes a two-headed arrow delineated by a thin line.
To amend the width of a single column or many columns, select them with the mouse and drag them in one of two directions: right or left.
Choose the rows you want to modify the height of, and then enter your new values.
Then, position the cursor underneath the chosen row heading or heads in the space between the row headers.
When the mouse is in the right spot, it becomes a two-headed arrow delineated by a thin line.
The chosen row or rows' height may be modified by clicking and dragging the handle up or down.
By selecting the columns, you want to modify, the width of those columns will be automatically adapted to fit the data.
The next step is to position the mouse cursor between the chosen column titles to a right of a chosen column title.
When the mouse is in the right spot, it becomes a two-headed arrow delineated by a thin line.
Then, double-click that area to make room for the biggest entries in the specified columns.
Select the rows you want to modify, and then press the AutoFit Height button.
Then, position the cursor underneath the chosen row heading or heads in the space between the row headers.
When the mouse is in the right spot, it becomes a two-headed arrow delineated by a thin line.
Double-clicking that location will instantly make the chosen rows taller to fit the tallest entries.

5.5 Selecting a Cell

You must first select the cell to add data into a cell or alter existing information.

- Simply clicking on a cell will choose it for you. In this instance, cell D9 will serve as an illustration.
- The selected cell will be highlighted, and a border will appear around it. In addition, the column and row titles will be highlighted. Within a worksheet, the cell that is now selected will remain selected until you click on another cell within the worksheet.

4	Department	First Name	Last Name	User Name	Part 1	Part 2
5	Sales	Walter	Rivera	wrivera	X	X
6	Sales	Heidi	Lee		X	X
7	Claims	Josie	Gates		X	X
8	Accounting	Wendy	Crocker		X	X
9	Accounting	Loretta	Johnson	⬚	X	
10	Sales	Walter	Rivera		X	
11	Claims	Misty	Whitfield		X	
12	Marketing	Matilda	Lewis		X	
13	Accounting	Elizabeth	Hicks		X	
14	HR	Alvin	Rios		X	
15	HR	Brian	Gaines		X	
16	Sales	Megan	Bosworth		X	
17	Claims	Maria	Menzies		X	
18	Claims	Micheal	Russell		X	
19						

You may also choose cells by using the arrow keys on your keyboard.
To select the cell range:
Several circumstances in which a cell range or a larger number of cells might prove beneficial.

- To select all the cells near one another, click and drag your mouse until the cells get highlighted. In this example, cells B 5 through C 18 will be used.
- Simply let go of the button on the mouse will allow you to choose a cell range. When you choose a cell in a worksheet, it will remain selected until you select a new cell from inside the same worksheet.

4	Department	First Name	Last Name	User Name	Part 1	Part 2
5	Sales	Walter	Rivera	wrivera	X	X
6	Sales	Heidi	Lee		X	X
7	Claims	Josie	Gates		X	X
8	Accounting	Wendy	Crocker		X	X
9	Accounting	Loretta	Johnson		X	
10	Sales	Walter	Rivera		X	
11	Claims	Misty	Whitfield		X	
12	Marketing	Matilda	Lewis		X	
13	Accounting	Elizabeth	Hicks		X	
14	HR	Alvin	Rios		X	
15	HR	Brian	Gaines		X	
16	Sales	Megan	Bosworth		X	
17	Claims	Maria	Menzies		X	
18	Claims	Micheal	Russell		X	
19						

5.6 Cutting, Copying, and Pasting Cells

Excel gives you the option to clip & paste information that has been entered into your spreadsheet, saving you both time and effort.

- Choosing the cell or cells you want to copy from your spreadsheet. As an example, you will use the number 9.
-

- You can copy something by pressing Ctrl and C on your keyboard, or you may utilize the Copy option on your home tab.

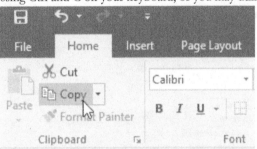

Click on the cells you want to enter your information to determine which ones they are. In this instance, you will choose option F 12: F 17. A box with dashes will appear around the cells that have been copied.

- After selecting Paste from the Home tab, hit the Ctrl and V keys simultaneously if you use a keyboard shortcut.

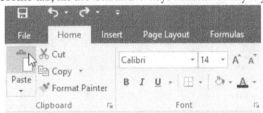

- The selected cells will have their respective contents inserted into them.

	Department	First Name	Last Name	User Name	Part 1	Part 2		Part 3
4								
5	Sales	Walter	Rivera	wrivera	X	X	On hold	X
6	Sales	Heidi	Lee		X	X	On hold	
7	Claims	Josie	Gates		X	X		X
8	Accounting	Wendy	Crocker		X	X		
9	Accounting	Loretta	Johnson		X	X		X
10	Claims	Misty	Whitfield		X			
11	Marketing	Matilda	Lewis		X			
12	Accounting	Elizabeth	Hicks		X	X		X
13	HR	Alvin	Rios		X	X		
14	HR	Brian	Gaines		X	X		
15	Sales	Megan	Bosworth		X	X		
16	Claims	Maria	Menzies		X	X		
17	Claims	Micheal	Russell		X	X		
18								
19								

To access the additional paste option:
When working with cells that include equations or formatting, you can also access other paste alternatives. To see all these different options, you must choose Paste from the menu and click the arrow next to the drop-down menu.

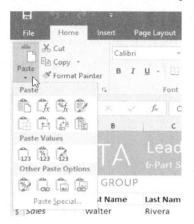

You may get quick access to instructions by avoiding the Ribbon and utilizing the right mouse button instead. To format a cell, right-click on the cell you want to format and choose "format" from the context menu. The drop-down menu may include commands that are already shown on the Ribbon.

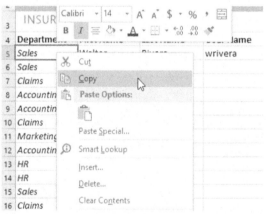

To cut & paste the cell content:
Instead of copying and pasting the information, it is possible to move it across other cells.

- To cut a cell, choose the cell you want to cut (s). As an example, you will utilize G 5: G 6.
- Choose Cut from the submenu that appears when you right-click the mouse. You may alternatively use the shortcut Ctrl+X on your keyboard, or you could choose "Command" from the menu on the home tab.

	Department	First Name	Last Name	User Name	Part 1	Part 2	
4							
5	Sales	Walter	Rivera	wrivera	X	X	On hold
6	Sales	Heidi	Lee		X	X	On hold
7	Claims	Josie	Gates		X	X	
8	Accounting	Wendy	Crocker		X	X	
9	Accounting	Loretta	Johnson		X	X	
10	Claims	Misty	Whitfield		X		
11	Marketing	Matilda	Lewis		X		
12	Accounting	Elizabeth	Hicks		X	X	
13	HR	Alvin	Rios		X	X	
14	HR	Brian	Gaines		X	X	
15	Sales	Megan	Bosworth		X	X	
16	Claims	Maria	Menzies		X	X	
17	Claims	Micheal	Russell		X	X	

Copy and paste the content into the cells that you have selected. You will begin by selecting F10:F11 as your starting point. A box with dashes will now be drawn around the cells that have been cut.
Create a copy of the text that is now chosen, and then paste it. You may alternatively use the shortcut Ctrl+V on your keyboard, or you could click the command button above the home tab.

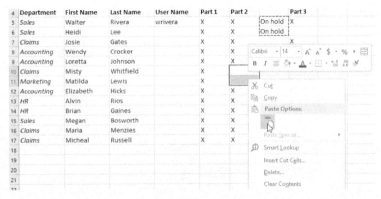

It is expected that the copied text will be pasted into the newly selected cells, after which the old cells will be cleared out.

Department	First Name	Last Name	User Name	Part 1	Part 2	Part 3
5 Sales	Walter	Rivera	wrivera	X	X	X
6 Sales	Heidi	Lee		X	X	
7 Claims	Josie	Gates		X	X	X
8 Accounting	Wendy	Crocker		X	X	
9 Accounting	Loretta	Johnson		X	X	X
10 Claims	Misty	Whitfield		X	On hold	
11 Marketing	Matilda	Lewis		X	On hold	
12 Accounting	Elizabeth	Hicks		X	X	
13 HR	Alvin	Rios		X	X	
14 HR	Brian	Gaines		X	X	
15 Sales	Megan	Bosworth		X	X	
16 Claims	Maria	Menzies		X	X	
17 Claims	Micheal	Russell		X	X	
18						

5.7 Keeping Headings Visible

When working with data included in a table, the header for each column will often be located at the very top of the table. No difficulty here.

	A	B	C	D	E
1	First Name	Last Name	Company	Address	City
2	James	Butt	Benton, John B Jr	6649 N Blue Gum St	New Orleans
3	Josephine	Darakjy	Chanay, Jeffrey A Esq	4 B Blue Ridge Blvd	Brighton
4	Art	Venere	Chemel, James L Cpa	8 W Cerritos Ave #54	Bridgeport
5	Lenna	Paprocki	Feltz Printing Service	639 Main St	Anchorage
6	Donette	Foller	Printing Dimensions	34 Center St	Hamilton
7	Simona	Morasca	Chapman, Ross E Esq	3 Mcauley Dr	Ashland
8	Mitsue	Tollner	Morlong Associates	7 Eads St	Chicago
9	Leota	Dilliard	Commercial Press	7 W Jackson Blvd	San Jose

However, if a significant row number extends much beyond the viewable page, you will need to scroll, & when you do, the header will no longer be visible.

	A	B	C	D	E
7	Simona	Morasca	Chapman, Ross E Esq	3 Mcauley Dr	Ashland
8	Mitsue	Tollner	Morlong Associates	7 Eads St	Chicago
9	Leota	Dilliard	Commercial Press	7 W Jackson Blvd	San Jose
10	Sage	Wieser	Truhlar And Truhlar Attys	5 Boston Ave #88	Sioux Falls
11	Kris	Marrier	King, Christopher A Esq	228 Runamuck Pl #2808	Baltimore
12	Minna	Amigon	Dorl, James J Esq	2371 Jerrold Ave	Kulpsville
13	Abel	Maclead	Rangoni Of Florence	37275 St Rt 17m M	Middle Island
14	Kiley	Caldarera	Feiner Bros	25 E 75th St #69	Los Angeles
15	Graciela	Ruta	Buckley Miller & Wright	98 Connecticut Ave Nw	Chagrin Falls

In this situation, the header may remain fixed (unmoved) at the top. Learn the steps here.

Keep header visible

You'll need to see the heading at the very top of the spreadsheet.

Select View from the Ribbon's tabs.

Just use the Freeze Panes icon within the Window menu.

You may freeze the top row by selecting the third button.

Wheel your mouse around. The header is now permanently displayed.

	A	B	C	D	E
1	First Name	Last Name	Company	Address	City
11	Kris	Marrier	King, Christopher A Esq	228 Runamuck Pl #2808	Baltimore
12	Minna	Amigon	Dorl, James J Esq	2371 Jerrold Ave	Kulpsville
13	Abel	Maclead	Rangoni Of Florence	37275 St Rt 17m M	Middle Island
14	Kiley	Caldarera	Feiner Bros	25 E 75th St #69	Los Angeles
15	Graciela	Ruta	Buckley Miller & Wright	98 Connecticut Ave Nw	Chagrin Falls
16	Cammy	Albares	Rousseaux, Michael Esq	56 E Morehead St	Laredo
17	Mattie	Poquette	Century Communications	73 State Road 434 E	Phoenix
18	Meaghan	Garufi	Bolton, Wilbur Esq	69734 E Carrillo St	Mc Minnville

You may unfreeze the top pane by selecting View ➔ Window ➔ Freeze Panes from the menu bar. Unfreeze Panes has replaced Freeze Panes at the pinnacle.

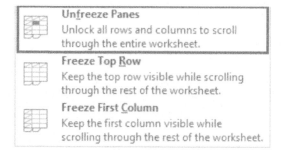

When you choose this, your worksheet will return to its previous state. The header has been defrosted and is available once more.

Chapter 6: Five Ways Excel Can Improve Productivity During Your Work from Home

There will be no retirement of Microsoft Excel. Spreadsheet software is widely used in workplaces all over the globe for a wide variety of purposes, including data analysis and organizing. Therefore, it is among the most crucial resources for any expert.
But you might not know that Excel may also be a major driver of efficiency. You may need each edge you can get when working from your home throughout a lockdown. Excel may provide just that.

6.1 Processing Large Amounts of Data

You deal with big volumes of data in your job as an account manager or data analyst. Excel is a wonderful tool for working with the massive amounts of data that are ubiquitous in today's world. Excel facilitates data processing with features such as pivot tables. By quickly rearranging categories, a pivot table facilitates the transformation of raw data into easily digestible tables. You can speed up creating useful business insights and save time doing it.

6.2 Utilizing Fill Handles

When populating tables using formulae, it's common practice to just repeat the formula across all rows. If you are familiar with Excel's data-navigation shortcuts, you can copy and paste a complete column of formulae with a few keystrokes. But using fill handles is much quicker since there's no need to scroll down to the table's actual data. In Excel, the rectangle in the bottom right corner of the selection represents the fill handle. If a formula is in a column adjacent to a column that already has data, you may easily copy the formula down to the bottom of a table by double-clicking the fill handle. Because of this, you can quickly and easily generate massive spreadsheets.

6.3 Examining Formulas All at Once

Excel will show you the formula in place of the result whenever you modify a cell that includes a formula. With the shortcut "Control +," you may see each formula in a worksheet at once. In a flash, you may modify any number of formulae using this handy quick cut. This is a fantastic method for checking the precision and readability of your document.

6.4 Leverage the Goal Seek Formula

The Excel feature "Goal Seek" helps you analyze the effects of changing one variable in a calculation on the others. You can rapidly examine the consequence of a change to a single cell input, making it a helpful tool for answering "what if" queries. This is particularly helpful in financial, sales, and forecasting situations where the adjustment of a single variable may significantly impact the results. To utilize it, just go to a cell and click the "What If Analysis" & "Goal Seek" buttons.

6.5 Automate Recurring Responsibilities With VBA

One of Excel's best features is the Virtual Basic for Applications (VBA). If you're accustomed to spending hours keying in the same data again, VBA can automate that process and reduce it to minutes. Whether you're putting in hours at the workplace or the house, this may be a tremendous help.

6.6 Best Excel Templates to Increase or Boost Your Productivity

Excel has proven to be an invaluable tool in enterprises and offices throughout the globe. Because of its adaptability and versatility may be used for various purposes and can help you do more in less time.
Excel's many time-saving and labor-enhancing features and functions are only the beginning. You may discover a variety of work management & company chart templates devoted to whatever job you have in mind, whether it's budgeting, task allocation, expenditure monitoring, etc.
Improve efficiency at work and ensure the smooth operation of your company by using one of the Excel templates provided here.
Business Plan Template
Despite being one of the most challenging and time-consuming things to do, having a well-thought-out business plan is central to the success of every organization. A business plan details all aspects of the company, from the products and services offered to the sales and marketing tactics, distribution plans, financial forecasts, and more.
Writing a business plan from scratch is daunting, particularly if you are inexperienced and lack the necessary writing abilities.

Budgeting Template

A manual budgeting process is fraught with difficulties, as anybody who has attempted it will attest. Managing a household budget is difficult enough without adding further mental strain by doing calculations.

Excel is a great tool for creating a budget and saving time on the arduous work of calculating numbers, but there is an even more time-saving alternative: budget templates.

Invoice Tracking Template

It may be a headache to go through thousands of invoices to determine which ones have been paid & which ones have not. Yet, if you don't maintain tabs on your collections, you'll be losing money.

This handy tracking template saves you the time and frustration of reviewing invoices individually. The spreadsheet should be used to record and track all invoice information, which should be added to and updated as appropriate after each time an invoice is sent to a client. Thanks to this standardized invoice, you'll never be late with a payment again.

Sales Goal Tracker Templates

To spot patterns and make necessary adjustments, businesses must monitor their sales activity. An effective sales monitoring spreadsheet is a valuable tool for any organization, whether you're looking to boost revenue or just keep tabs on operations.

Schedule Templates

Time management is as crucial as financial accounting for the success of any business. If you waste time, it's gone forever; therefore, it's important to prioritize how you use it.

Free Company Schedule Templates are available on Schedule Templates if you're a small business owner without access to a dedicated HR department. Put these schedule templates to use to create and keep a timetable that will help your business thrive.

World Meeting Planners

Nowadays, individuals from all over the globe may work together remotely, contribute to projects, and keep a company operating smoothly. This methodology is effective in many ways, but it may be difficult to coordinate conferences and meeting calls when team members are in various time zones. Here's when the global meeting planner template is useful.

Use this schedule when coordinating a meeting with up to six persons in various time zones. After inputting the UTC offsets and Daylight-Saving Time (DST) guidelines for your international business partners or staff, the spreadsheet will indicate whether the proposed meeting time is convenient for everyone.

In addition to the various ways, it may be used to increase efficiency in the office, Excel also has a broad range of other applications. If you know what you're doing, you may save a lot of time and effort by making use of premade Excel templates.

Chapter 7: Relative, Absolute, and Mixed Cell References in Excel

Each cell on an Excel spreadsheet has a specific purpose. You may refer to these cells by entering the row and column numbers.

For instance, the coordinates A1 would denote the first cell in the first row (1st) and the 1st column (specified as A). A similar notation, B3, would refer to the third column of the second row.

Excel's strength comes from the fact that you can incorporate these cell references into your formulae.

At present, Excel supports three distinct forms of cell reference:

- Relative Cell Reference
- Absolute Cell Reference
- Mixed Cell Reference

Being familiar with these cell reference types will make working with formulae easier and more efficient (especially if copy-pasting formulas).

7.1 What Are Relative Cell References in Excel?

First, let's use a basic scenario to clarify what you mean by "related cell references" in Excel.

Assume the following data set exists:

	A	B	C	D
1	**Item**	**Price**	**Quantity**	**Total**
2	Item A	15	15	
3	Item B	20	20	
4	Item C	12	18	
5	Item D	18	8	
6	Item E	8	10	
7	Item F	10	20	
8	Item G	20	10	

Each item's total is arrived at by multiplying its unit price by its unit amount.

To calculate the first item, just enter the formula B 2*C 2 into cell D 2:

| D2 | | fx | =B2*C2 | |

	A	B	C	D
1	**Item**	**Price**	**Quantity**	**Total**
2	Item A	15	15	225
3	Item B	20	20	
4	Item C	12	18	
5	Item D	18	8	
6	Item E	8	10	
7	Item F	10	20	
8	Item G	20	10	

Instead of manually putting the formula into each cell, you can now just copy cell D 2 & paste this into the rest of the cells (D 3: D 8). After you do so, you'll see the cell reference update to point to the correct row. The formula in cell D3 is changed to B 3 * C 3, whereas the formula in cell D 4 is changed to B 4 * C 4.

| D2 | | fx | =B2*C2 | |

	A	B	C	D
1	**Item**	**Price**	**Quantity**	**Total**
2	Item A	15	15	225
3	Item B	20	20	
4	Item C	12	18	
5	Item D	18	8	
6	Item E	8	10	
7	Item F	10	20	

| D3 | | fx | | |

	A	B	C	D
1	**Item**	**Price**	**Quantity**	**Total**
2	Item A	15	15	225
3	Item B	20	20	
4	Item C	12	18	
5	Item D	18	8	
6	Item E	8	10	
7	Item F	10	20	

| D3 | | fx | =B3*C3 | |

	A	B	C	D
1	**Item**	**Price**	**Quantity**	**Total**
2	Item A	15	15	225
3	Item B	20	20	400
4	Item C	12	18	216
5	Item D	18	8	144
6	Item E	8	10	80
7	Item F	10	20	200

In Excel, such references are referred to as relative cell references since they update automatically whenever the cell is copied.
When Should you Use Excel's Relative Cell References?
When formulating for a set of cells, referring to neighboring cells by their respective cell references might be helpful.
The formula may then be created in one cell and pasted into the others.

7.2 Excel Absolute Cell Reference

Not like relative cell reference, absolute cell reference remain unchanged when the formula is copied to all other cells.
Consider the data set below, in which you must determine the commission for the sum of sales of each item.
Cell G1 contains a commission rate of 20%.

	A	B	C	D	E	F	G
1	**Item**	**Price**	**Quantity**	**Total**	**Commission**		20%
2	Item A	15	15	225			
3	Item B	20	20	400			
4	Item C	12	18	216			
5	Item D	18	8	144			
6	Item E	8	10	80			
7	Item F	10	20	200			
8	Item G	20	10	200			

Just use the following formula into cell E 2 & paste it along the column to determine the commission for every item sold:
=D 2 * G1

E2			fx	=D2*G1			

	A	B	C	D	E	F	G
1	**Item**	**Price**	**Quantity**	**Total**	**Commission**		20%
2	Item A	15	15	225	45		
3	Item B	20	20	400	80		
4	Item C	12	18	216	43.2		
5	Item D	18	8	144	28.8		
6	Item E	8	10	80	16		
7	Item F	10	20	200	40		
8	Item G	20	10	200	40		

Remember that the cell reference G2 contains the commission, which includes two-dollar signs ($).
What is the purpose of the dollar symbol ($)?
Adding the dollar sign ($) before the row and column number makes it an absolute reference (i.e., stops column and row number from altering when copied into other cells).
When You duplicate a formula from the cell E 2 to E 3, for instance, it becomes =D3*G1 rather than =D2*G1.
Remember that although D2 becomes D3, G1 remains the same.
Placing the ($) dollar sign head of the "G" and "1" in G1 prevents the cell reference from changing when the cell is cloned.
As a result, the cell coordinates are unquestionable.
When Should You Use Excel's Absolute Cell References?
It is helpful to utilize absolute cell references when you don't want the formula's cell reference to altering when you copy and paste it from one location to another. This could occur if the formula calls for a certain predetermined value (such as commission rate, tax rate, months number, etc.)
You could simply substitute 20 % for G2 in the calculation but keeping the value in a cell & referencing it would enable you to modify it whenever you choose.
If the commission structure were to change so that you were paying out 25 % instead of 20 %, all the calculations would be updated by just altering the number in cell G 2.

7.3 What Are Mixed Cell References in Excel?

Unlike relative and absolute cell references, mixed cell references might be confusing.
Referencing a cell that has both forms of information is possible in two ways:

- When a formula is copied, just the column is updated, but the original row remains unchanged.
- The row is modified when a formula is duplicated, but the corresponding column remains locked.

Let's look at a concrete example to understand how it works.
The percentages in cells E2, F2, & G2 of the following data set will be used to determine the three commission levels.

	A	B	C	D	E	F	G
1					**Commission**		
2					**10%**	**15%**	**20%**
3	**Item**	**Price**	**Quantity**	**Total**	**Tier 1**	**Tier 2**	**Tier 3**
4	Item A	15	15	225			
5	Item B	20	20	400			
6	Item C	12	18	216			
7	Item D	18	8	144			
8	Item E	8	10	80			
9	Item F	10	20	200			
10	Item G	20	10	200			

With the help of mixed references, it is now possible to utilize a single formula to determine all these commissions.
Put the formula below into cell E4, and then paste it into all other cells.

=$B4*$C4*E$2

| E4 | | ▼ | : | × | ✓ | fx | =$B4*$C4*E$2 |

	A	B	C	D	E	F	G
1						Commission	
2					10%	15%	20%
3	Item	Price	Quantity	Total	Tier 1	Tier 2	Tier 3
4	Item A	15	15	225	22.5	33.75	45
5	Item B	20	20	400	40	60	80
6	Item C	12	18	216	21.6	32.4	43.2
7	Item D	18	8	144	14.4	21.6	28.8
8	Item E	8	10	80	8	12	16
9	Item F	10	20	200	20	30	40
10	Item G	20	10	200	20	30	40

Both types of mixed cell references are used in the calculation (one where the row is locked & one where the column is locked). Let's go out every cell reference and figure out how it functions:

- $B4 ($C4) – The dollar symbol appears immediately before the Column notation, but not the Row number in this citation. Since the column is fixed, the reference will stay the same when you transfer the formula to a cell to the right. If you duplicate the formula from cell E4 to cell F4, this reference will remain the same. If you were to write it down, the row number might shift as you copied it.
- E$2 – The dollar symbol appears before the row number, although it is absent from the column notation. With the row number fixed, the formula may be copied without worrying about the reference changing as you go down the sheet. The column alphabet is not locked; thus, if you duplicate the formula to a right, it will change.

7.4 How to Change the Reference from Relative to Absolute (or Mixed)?

Putting a dollar sign in front of column notation & row number makes the reference absolute.
For instance, the cell reference A1 is relative, but if you change it to A1, it will become absolute.
Making the changes one by one could be simple if you have a few references to modify. To adjust the formula, click on the formula bar (select a cell, press F2, & change it).
It's also feasible to do this rapidly by pressing the F4 key on your keyboard.
The reference will be updated if you hit F4 after selecting a cell reference (either within formula bar or the cell itself in edit mode).
Let's pretend you have the formula =A1 inside a cell.
To see the result of selecting the reference and pressing F4, please see the following.

- Press the F4 key once: By switching to absolute notation, the cell reference moves from A1 to A1.
- Press the F4 key 2 times: Instead of referring to cell A1, you would now use cell A$1 (alterations to the mixed reference wherever a row is locked).
- Press the F4 key 3 times: The A1 cell reference becomes the $A1 cell reference (changes to the mixed reference wherever the column is locked).
- Press the F4 key 4 times: The cell number is reset to A1.

7.5 Multiplication Table Utilizing Mixed References

In this session, you will discover the tricks and tips for making multiplication in Excel and Google Sheets.

| C4 | | ▼ | : | × | ✓ | fx | =$B4*C$3 | | | | | | | |

	A	B	C	D	E	F	G	H	I	J	K	L	M
1		Multiplication Table											
3			1	2	3	4	5	6	7	8	9	10	
4		1	1	2	3	4	5	6	7	8	9	10	
5		2	2	4	6	8	10	12	14	16	18	20	
6		3	3	6	9	12	15	18	21	24	27	30	
7		4	4	8	12	16	20	24	28	32	36	40	
8		5	5	10	15	20	25	30	35	40	45	50	
9		6	6	12	18	24	30	36	42	48	54	60	
10		7	7	14	21	28	35	42	49	56	63	70	
11		8	8	16	24	32	40	48	56	64	72	80	
12		9	9	18	27	36	45	54	63	72	81	90	
13		10	10	20	30	40	50	60	70	80	90	100	

Sheet1 ⊕

Setting up the Data
To begin, populate Rows A2 through A11 with the numbers 1 through 10, and then Rows B1 through K1 with the same numbers.

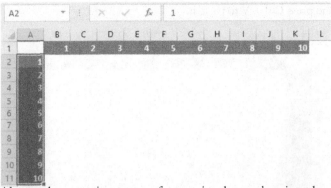

The TRANSPOSE function provides another engaging strategy for entering the numbers into the cells:

- In the range from A2 to A11, type the digits 1 through 10.
- The following formula should be entered into the formula bar and applied to the cells in the range B1:K1.
- To utilize this formula, you must enter an array by pressing Ctrl+Shift+Enter.

=TRANSPOSE(A2:A11)

The foundation for your multiplication chart is complete. Two methods of filling up the multiplication table are shown below.

Multiplication Table with mixed references

The multiplication table could be generated utilizing mixed cell references—where one row or column reference is protected while the additional is not.

The formula for cell B 2:

= $A2*B$1

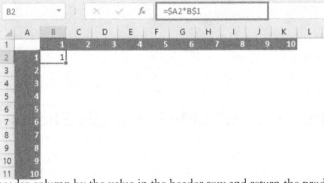

This will multiply the row in the header column by the value in the header row and return the product.

Finally, you'll fill up the complete range using this formula:

- Copy the cell B 2 (Ctrl + C).
- Selecting the range B 2: K 11

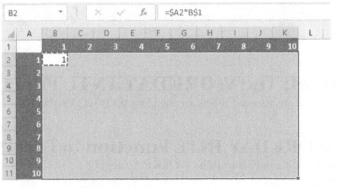

- Just copy the formula and press Ctrl + V to paste it.

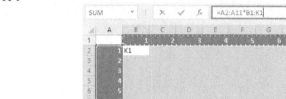

7.6 Multiplication Table Utilizing an Array Formula

The use of array formulas is also a straightforward approach.
The following formula may be inserted into the formula bar by selecting the range B1:K1 and then pressing Ctrl+Shift+Enter:
=A 2: A 11*B 1: K 1

Through this process, the whole table of multiplication may be generated.

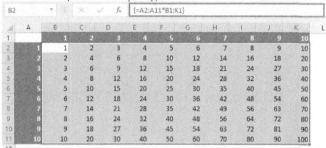

7.7 Create the Multiplication Table in Google Sheets

The formula for making a multiplication table is the same in Google Sheets as it is in Excel:

Chapter 8: MS Excel: The WORKDAY.INTL Function

In this chapter, you will go through advanced excel functions including WORKDAY.INTL function, RANDBETWEEN function and RAND function.

8.1 How to Use a WORKDAY.INTL Function in Excel?

You may get a rough completion date for a project by using WORKDAY.INTL.

This one is more adaptable than WORKDAY, which rigidly adhered to the notion that weekends were always on Sunday and Saturday. You have the option of picking various weekends or building your list.

WORKDAY.INTL Arguments

WORKDAY. INTL has a minimum requirement of two parameters and a maximum of four.

- **start_date:** the date on which one should begin the calculation.
- **Days:** The commencement date and the ending date are both considered to be whole days.
- **Weekend: (optional)** a unique identifier denotes the days that are working days.
- **Holidays: (optional)** days on the calendar that are currently not being used

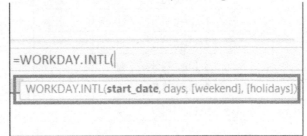

Notes regarding WORKDAY.INTL

The DAY ON THE JOB. There are several applications for the INTL function, including the following:

Start Date

Only the integer will be shown once the first digit of the current date has been eliminated.

If you submit anything like a time and date, for example, it won't be considered.

Pick a day that is also a working day for the most productive outcomes.

Days

You're going to reduce the number of days till it's as close as possible to an integer.

A number might have a positive, negative, or zero to indicate whether it is moving forward or backward. A return to the initial date is indicated by a value of zero.

Weekend

In this instance, it is not necessary. If they are not counted, Sunday and Saturday are days off from work.

To get things started, let's have a look at this problem:

- Choose from the list that appears below.
- It is also possible to generate a seven-digit array that contains one character that does not function and no characters that do work.

Holidays

- In this instance, it is not necessary. If calendar dates are disregarded, there are no days that are not considered working days.

Project End Date

The DAY ON THE JOB. In the above scenario, the INTL function might be used to calculate the completion date of a project. Like WORKDAY, but with the freedom to choose which days off to take.

Take, for instance:

- Start with the arguments about WORKDAY. The beginning date and number of days for INTL
- Then comes the task of buying Christmas presents.
- Finally, days off from work would be set aside.

Start with Basics

To start with WORKDAY, you will need two different pieces of information. Fundamental characteristics of the INTL function:

How much time do you predict it will take to finish the project?

The working day has begun!

INTL shall determine when the necessary length of time has elapsed from the commencement date to arrive at the actual date on which work will begin.

As the screenshot demonstrates, you start working on the project on Thursday, December 10th (cell C 8), and it will be finished in two days (cell C10).

The following WORKDAY is included in cell C12.

INTL formula:

=WORKDAY.INTL (C8, C10)

C12	=WORKDAY.INTL(C8,C10)

	A	B	C	D
7				
8		Project Start Date	Thu 10-Dec-15	
9				
10		Number of Days	2	
11				
12		**Project End Date**	**Mon 14-Dec-15**	
13				

Check your Calculation
See the subsequent table for an explanation of why December 14th was selected.
The project is given priority on Thursdays and Fridays so that work may be done on those days (2 days).
Since you didn't mention that you worked on weekends, it assumes that you don't do any work on Saturdays or Sundays.
The result of applying the algorithm was that the next working day fell on Monday, December 14th.

Date	Work?	Project Day
Thu 10-Dec-15	1	1
Fri 11-Dec-15	1	2
Sat 12-Dec-15	0	
Sun 13-Dec-15	0	
Mon 14-Dec-15	1	
Tue 15-Dec-15	1	

Adjust your End Date
You would want to know when the project is anticipated to be finished, as opposed to the next business day. To arrive at the required answer, you must remove one from the total number of days included in the computation.
=WORKDAY.INTL (C8, C10-1)
The project's completion date will thus be on Friday, December 11th.

C12	=WORKDAY.INTL(C8,C10-1)

	A	B	C	D
7				
8		Project Start Date	Thu 10-Dec-15	
9				
10		Number of Days	2	
11				
12		Project End Date	Fri 11-Dec-15	
13				

Exclude Holidays
You can ignore holidays while using the WORKDAY function, just as you did with its predecessor. INTL.
When working with a named Excel table, including, or excluding dates is simple. The Holiday List may be seen in the date column of the table tblHol in the figure below.

Enter a List of Holidays

Date	Holiday
26-Nov-2015	Thanksgiving
25-Dec-2015	Christmas
26-Dec-2015	Boxing Day
1-Jan-2016	New Year's Day

You will use the function's fourth argument to exclude holidays from date calculations.

=WORKDAY.INTL (C8, C10-1, tblHol [Date])

A project kicked off on the 24th of December and will end on the 28th of the same month.

	A	B	C
7			
8		Project Start Date	Thu 24-Dec-15
9			
10		Number of Days	2
11			
12		Project End Date	Mon 28-Dec-15
13			

The following is a table that details the working days and the holidays indicated in orange.

Date	Work?	Project Day
Thu 24-Dec-15	1	1
Fri 25-Dec-15	0	
Sat 26-Dec-15	0	
Sun 27-Dec-15	0	
Mon 28-Dec-15	1	2
Tue 29-Dec-15	1	

Specify your Non-Working Days

If you don't say, WORKDAY. INTL automatically disregards weekends and other non-working days. You are free to choose other days as weekends using either of the following methods:

- choose from the list
- 1 & 0 string

Select from the Drop-Down List

It is much easier to designate weekend days by selecting from a drop-down list of available alternatives. When you start the function using the third argument, the list will appear as soon as the function is started.
If you don't see the list, press Alt + Down Arrow to bring it up.

=WORKDAY.INTL(C8,C10-1,

E	
	1 - Saturday, Sunday
	2 - Sunday, Monday
	3 - Monday, Tuesday
	4 - Tuesday, Wednesday
	5 - Wednesday, Thursday
	6 - Thursday, Friday
	7 - Friday, Saturday
	11 - Sunday only
	12 - Monday only

Option 2, which takes place over the weekend and Monday, pushes the deadline for the project to the 29th of December.

=WORKDAY.INTL (C8, C10-1, 2, tblHol [Date])

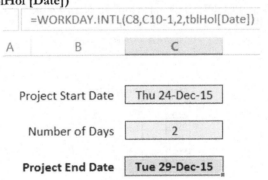

	=WORKDAY.INTL(C8,C10-1,2,tblHol[Date])

A	B	C
	Project Start Date	Thu 24-Dec-15
	Number of Days	2
	Project End Date	**Tue 29-Dec-15**

Create Non-Working Days String

If none of the options in the drop-down menu match your criteria, you will need to create your string.
The first seven numerals in the string stand in for each of the seven days of the week.
The number zero denotes the beginning of a workday.
Use a 1 for days that aren't considered working days.
If you only work Mondays, Wednesdays, and Fridays, you can get away with using the string 0101011.

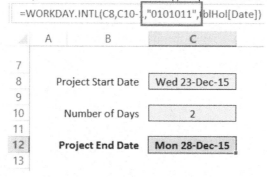

You will change the beginning date to 23rd December, a productive day in your new calendar. The revised formula may be seen below, and it now includes a 7-digit string encased in double quotation marks as the third argument.

=WORKDAY.INTL (C8, C10-1, "0101011", tblHol [Date])

As a direct consequence of these adjustments, the due date has been brought up and is now on Monday, December 28.

=WORKDAY.INTL(C8,C10-1,"0101011",tblHol[Date])

	A	B	C
7			
8		Project Start Date	Wed 23-Dec-15
9			
10		Number of Days	2
11			
12		**Project End Date**	**Mon 28-Dec-15**
13			

Calculate Non-Working String

The selection of days off from work could be simplified by using a table like the one that follows. You may denote days off from work by using an X, and an IF formula can be used to show either 0 or 1 in every row.

=IF (K8="x",1,0)

To compress the string into its final form, a CONCATENATE formula is used to it:
= CONCATENATE (M 8, M 9, M 10, M 11, M 12, M 13, M 14)

=CONCATENATE(M8,M9,M10, M11,M12,M13,M14)

Mark Non-Working Days

Day	Off	Day #	Calc
Mon		1	0
Tue	x	2	1
Wed		3	0
Thu	x	4	1
Fri		5	0
Sat	x	6	1
Sun	x	7	1
			0101011

Weekend string
for formula

Employ the contents of this cell as the value for the third parameter in the WORKDAY.INTL computation.
=WORKDAY.INTL (C 8, C 10-1, M 15, tblHol [Date])
You may have hidden a calculation column in your spreadsheet so that other people can't mess with the formula.
Nth Weekdays of the Month (WORKDAY. INTL)
THE WORKING DAY ITSELF One may get the Nth weekday of the month by using the INTL function in conjunction with a single individualized string of the days that are not considered working days.
Excel's WORKDAY.
By using the INTL function, find the weekday that corresponds to the Nth position inside a given month and year. To know when Canadians will celebrate Thanksgiving this year, check the calendar to discover which Monday comes after the first one in October.
Examples: The fourth Thursday of every November in the United States is Thanksgiving Day.
For example, the Thanksgiving holiday is always celebrated on the fourth Thursday of November in the United States.
The date of Thanksgiving may be calculated with the help of the formula that can be found in cell C10 of the graphic that can be seen below:
= WORKDAY.INTL (DATE (C 4, D 5, 0), C 7, "1110111")

Within a string of non-working days consisting of seven digits, one working day is present (Thursday).
As a result, the proper day to celebrate Thanksgiving is the fourth Thursday in November.

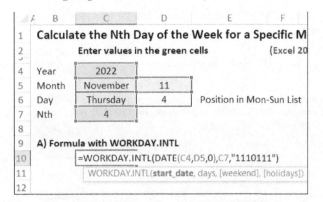

8.2 MS Excel: The RANDBETWEEN Function

A random integer will be generated by the RANDBETWEEN function depending on the integers supplied. This feature does its computations whenever the worksheet is opened or modified.

Following is a list of the parameters that are sent to the RANDBETWEEN function:

Down: (Required Function) This is the smallest possible number the function may return when it is called on the set.

In the set, the value denoted by "Peak" refers to the integer value that is capable of being produced by the "Mandatory Function."

Employing the RANDBETWEEN Function in a Sentence

Look at the table below to get a better idea of how the RANDBETWEEN function is use.

f_x =RANDBETWEEN(A2, B2)

	A	B	C	D
1	Bottom	Top	Result	
2	2	3	3	
3	3	10	4	
4	120	300	205	
5	32	121	102	

The RANDBETWEEN technique is now included in the table that was just shown to you. =RANDBETWEEN (A2, B2).

As seen in the table below, the worksheet output changes each time the equations in the table are used more than once.

f_x =RANDBETWEEN(A2, B2)

	A	B	C	D
1	Bottom	Top	Result	
2	2	3	2	
3	3	10	8	
4	120	300	181	
5	32	121	87	

When using the RANDBETWEEN tool, a few important factors must be kept in mind.

The RANDBETWEEN function will return a new value whenever the worksheet is amended, including tabulated.

Instead of using the F9 key to transform the model into its output, you should input the RANDBETWEEN function into the formula bar to prevent the random number from changing while the worksheet is generated.

A collection of random numbers may be generated in many cells by selecting a cell, inserting the RANDBETWEEN module, and then pressing Ctrl + Enter once the module has been inserted.

8.3 Excel RAND Function

Excel's RAND() function may be found under the Math & Trig section. It gives back a random number ranging from 0 & to 1. The range of this random number ranges from +1 to -1.

The outcome of this calculation is very variable since the Excel RAND() function doesn't accept any arguments. You may be questioning how & why this formula is employed.

Learn the ins and outs of the RAND() function, its features, and some instances of its use in this chapter. You'll also summarize the benefits of using this feature.

Syntax

It is a straightforward function that takes no arguments.

=RAND()

The result of the random number calculation, which ranges from 0 to 1, is then returned to the user.

Purpose

A random integer between 0 and 1 may be generated using the RAND() function. A recalculation of the time formula is performed whenever an Excel worksheet is opened or closed.

Specify range

You also can set your own range, within which a random number will be selected, and have it picked from within that range. Take, for instance:

=RAND () * (b - a) + a

The number b represents the highest value inside the set range, while the number a represents the lowest value.

Note that the random number returned by this function would never be higher than the maximum possible number.

Example,

=RAND () * (25 - 10) + 10

The algorithm shown above will produce a random number ranging from 10 to 24.9999.

We have compiled a collection of instances into a table for your perusal so that you may investigate the myriad of ways in which this function operates and the results it produces.

Formula	Result	Range
0.312225579	A random number between 0 to 1 excluding 1.	0 to 0.99999
16.76678914	A random number between 10 to 25.	10 to 24.9999
163.6888298	A random number chosen between greater than or equal to 100 and 200.	100 to 199.9999
=INT(RAND()* (200-100)+100))	A random integer number between 100 and 200. *It will not choose a float random number.*	100 to 199 (Only integer number will return).

On the other hand, the RANDBETWEEN() formula is another option for doing this task. Excel allows you to modify the RAND() function to meet your specific requirements and perform the same actions as RANDBETWEEN.

Why is this function needed?

A series of integers chosen at random is produced by the RAND() function. Excel users are frequently confronted with the necessity to delegate random tasks or numbers. You may do that by making use of this function.

It will be easier for users of Excel to delegate any random number or job to a group of individuals if they first assign each person a random number.

How to utilize RAND() function?

You need to learn the RAND() function using an example by deploying it to some data in Excel. This will help you understand where & how to utilize the function. You will provide two to three working examples of such a function to better understand its use.

In the next step, you will apply the RAND() method to the data in Excel. For this purpose, you have used this collection of numerical data.

RAND() implementation

First, you have not laid forth any requirements. In this workbook, you will only utilize the RAND() function. So, put pen to paper

=RAND()

Whenever you want, anywhere you want, on your Excel sheet.

Simple RAND() function with no additional data

Second, obtain the outcome by pressing the Enter key. This method gains a random integer among 0 & 1.

a random number between range 0 and 1

Your random number would vary each time you make an edit to the same Excel page, including insertions, deletions, and formatting changes.

After running RAND() again, you'll see that the outcome has changed.

Part 4: The random number returned by this method will change every time it is called. This will be a different number each time. Try to find a fresh random number -

The earlier outcome has shifted once again.

Chapter 9: MS Excel: The VLOOKUP Function

In this chapter, you will go through advanced excel functions including VLOOKUO function and HLOOKUP function.

9.1 How to Use VLOOKUP in Excel?

The VLOOKUP function searches for specific information inside the first column of a dataset or table and then returns that information from a different column located within the same row.

These values serve as the parameters for VLOOKUP:

=VLOOKUP (col_index_num, table_array, lookup_value, [range_lookup])

- **Look-up_value (Required argument):** The value that should be searched for in the first column of the table or dataset.
- **Table_array (Required argument):** the data array that the lookup value may seek inside the left-hand portion of the column's layout.
- **Col_index_num (Needed argument):** The returned statistics are represented in the table by integers or column numbers, depending on which one they are.
- **Range_lookup (optional argument):** Depending on how this piece of code is written, VLOOK can either find an exact match or a good one. The value of the statement might be either TRUE or FALSE, depending on the context. The next highest value is returned if a suitable match cannot be located. If no precise match is found, the error message #N/A is returned, while the value FALSE indicates that a match has been found.

Utilizing this function to determine the value of yam in the table may be done by following the steps that are stated below:

- Choose a blank cell, and then type in the cell that will serve as your lookup value method. This is the cell that has the data that you want. In this scenario, the lookup cell is A12, and its formula is as follows: Yam = VLOOKUP (A12)

9.2 VLOOKUP in Financial Modeling and Financial Analysis

To make financial models increasingly dynamic and encompass numerous situations, the VLOOKUP formula is often utilized. Consider a financial model with a debt timetable, where the corporation considered three interest rate outcomes (3.0%, 4.00%, and 5.00%). Interest rates for low, medium, & high scenarios might be input into the spreadsheet using a VLOOKUP.

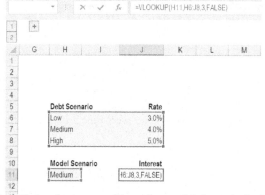

The interest rate for the selected scenario will then be imported into the model through the VLOOKUP formula, as seen above.

9.3 Things to remember about the VLOOKUP Function

Microsoft Excel VLOOKUP Formula is described here, along with some key points to keep in mind:

- In the absence of range lookup, VLOOKUP will accept a fuzzy match, but it would prioritize an excellent fit if one is available.
- The function always produces correct visual results is its primary drawback. Information will be retrieved from the table rows that follow the first column to the right.
- VLOOKUP will only find a match for the first value in the lookup column if it includes duplicates.
- The case is irrelevant to the function.
- Let's pretend a VLOOKUP formula already exists in your spreadsheet. There is a risk that the formulae may become invalid if you add a new column to the table. This is the case since manually updated column index values are not updated when new columns are added or existing ones are removed.
- A wildcard character, like an asterisk (*) or question mark (?), may be used in a VLOOKUP.
- Let's pretend the numbers in the function were inserted into the table you're dealing with as text. To be honest, it doesn't matter if all you're doing is obtaining textual numbers from a table field. A #N/A! error will occur if the lookup value isn't also throughout the text form and the initial column of the table includes numbers input as text.
- If your VLOOKUP function returns an error code of #N/A! The lookup will be considered unsuccessful when it cannot locate a value matching the one provided in the lookup value argument.
- If the col index num parameter is more than the number of columns inside the table array provided, a #REF! An error will occur.
- A reference to your cell that does not exist was made in the formula.
- If the col index num argument becomes less than one or cannot be converted to a numeric value, or if the range lookup parameter cannot be converted to a logical value of TRUE or FALSE, then a #VALUE! An error will be generated.

9.4 MS Excel: the HLOOKUP Function

The HLOOKUP function, which stands for "horizontal lookup," is a device that can retrieve a value or a piece of information from the top row of a table array or dataset and return it along with another row's given value or item in the same column. The HLOOKUP function is referred to by its acronym, which stands for "horizontal lookup."
The HLOOKUP function requires the following information as input to do its tasks.
(Value lookup, table array, row index number, and lookup range) = HLOOKUP
To get your total score in Joy in Mathematics, just compute it by following the guidelines below.
Choose an empty cell, and then the lookup value or the cell containing the data that must be searched for should be entered.

- In this scenario, the search cell is B1, where the name is stored. Pleasure; =HLOOKUP (B1

	A	B	C	D	E	F	G
1	STUDENT SCORES	JOY	LOVETH	JOHN	ADE X		
2	MATHEMATICS	59	45	68	93		
3	ENGLISH	69	78	43	75		
4	ECONOMICS	34	56	65	89		
5	PHE	23	89	24	97		
6							
7	THE TOTAL SCORE OF JOY IN MATHEMATICS	=HLOOKUP(B1					
8		HLOOKUP(lookup_value, table_array, row_index_num, [range_lookup])					

To conclude, you may tell Excel whether you're searching for an exact match or an excellent fit by choosing TRUE or FALSE from the drop-down menu.
= HLOOKUP (B1, A1:E5,3, FALSE) or =HLOOKUP (B1, A1:E5,3, TRUE)

	A	B	C	D	E	F	G
		✕ ✓ fx	=HLOOKUP(B1, A1:E5,2, FALSE)				
1	STUDENT SCORES	JOY	LOVETH	JOHN	ADE X		
2	MATHEMATICS	59	45	68	98		
3	ENGLISH	69	78	43	76		
4	ECONOMICS	34	56	65	89		
5	PHE	23	89	24	97		
6							
7	THE TOTAL SCORE OF JOY IN MATHEMATICS	=HLOOKUP(B1, A1:E5,2, FALSE)					
8		HLOOKUP(lookup_value, table_array, row_index_num, [range_lookup])					

9.5 Tips for HLOOKUP Function

You may ignore the case while searching. The system will treat the words "TIM" and "tim" as interchangeable.
When using HLOOKUP, the 'Lookup value' should be the first entry in the 'table array'. If you need to broaden your search, you'll have to develop a new Excel formula.
The 'lookup value' input to HLOOKUP (only if 'lookup value' is text) may include wildcard characters like '*' or '?'.
Let's look at an illustration to see what You mean.
Let's pretend the list of student names and grades below is real:

Student name	Amy	Brain	Cathy	Donald	Ela
Accounts	75	65	70	60	59
Economics	65	72	78	89	67
Management	70	68	90	72	58
Mathematics	80	90	75	65	87

To utilize the Parallel Lookup formula to locate a student's Math grades whose last name begins with the letter 'D,' the formula would read as follows:

Fetch Marks of D in Management	=HLOOKUP("D*",A12:F16,5,FALSE)
	HLOOKUP(lookup_value, table_array, row_index_num, [range_lookup])

The asterisk (*) is used as the wildcard.
If your 'range lookup' is put to FALSE & the HLOOKUP function is unable to locate the 'lookup value' inside the specified range, the #N/A error is returned. Putting the function within IFERROR allows you to customize the error message shown. For instance, =IFERROR (HLOOKUP (A 4, A 1: I 2, 2, FALSE), "No value found") displays the custom error message.
Fifth, HLOOKUP would throw a #VALUE! Error if the 'row index num' was less than 1. Row indexes that are more than the total quantity of columns in the table array will result in a #REF! Error.
Keep in mind that the Excel HLOOKUP function will only return one result. If the lookup value is n, this is the first number n that matches. What if a small number of rows in the table are duplicates? Using a Pivot table, you should either eliminate them or put them in separate groups. The array formula may remove all duplicate values in the lookup range from the Pivot table.

Chapter 10: MS Excel: the TRANSPOSE Function (WS)

In this chapter, you will go through advanced excel functions including TRANSPOSE function and COUNTBLANK function.

10.1 How to use the TRANSPOSE Function in Excel?

A spectrum or array may be flipped using the TRANSPOSE operator. Alterations are made to both the vertical and horizontal ranges.
There is just one parameter for TRANSPOSE. =Transpose (array)
Choose the blank cells. Check if the numbers in the selected cells are identical to the first set.

- In the selected blanks cells, type =**TRANSPOSE**

Cells should be transposed into their natural habitat.

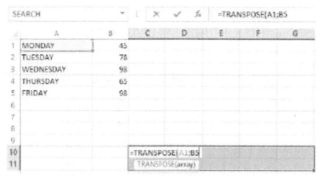

The cell range may be transposed by pressing CTRL+SHIFT+ENTER.

10.2 MS Excel: The COUNTBLANK Function

Excel's STATISTICAL functions include COUNTBLANK [1]. The COUNTBLANK function calculates the sum of blank cells in a range.

In the case of financial analysis, the function may either count or highlight empty cells.

Formula

=COUNTBLANK (range)

Where:

The range specifies which cells are blank.

Regarding the COUNTBLANK function: This function does not count text, numbers, typos, or anything else.

Even empty formulae ("") are counted in this exercise. A cell is blank by COUNTBLANK if it includes a blank text string and a formula that produces a single value.

Cells that are filled with zeros are not considered to be blank.

Using COUNTBLANK Function within Excel?

In the formula of a cell in a worksheet, you may make use of the COUNTBLANK function. Examine an example to get an understanding of the function's many uses.

COUNTBLANK Example

Conditional formatting is used in this approach to conduct the counting of empty cells.

Take into consideration the following information:

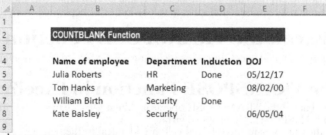

=COUNTBLANK (A2:D5) is used to count empty rows.

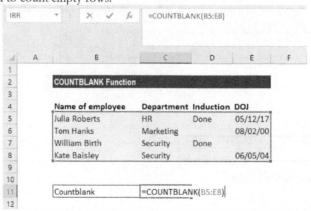

Gil B. Dreher

Results:

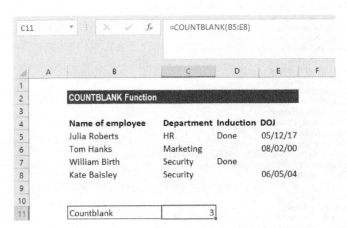

You can highlight rows that include empty cells by using conditional formatting and the COUNTBLANK function. After selecting the necessary range, apply the conditional formatting using the COUNTBLANK() function. This draws attention to all the blank cells inside the range.

Chapter 11: Convert Numbers into Words

If you've got a column of numeric numbers in a worksheet, & you now need to convert those numeric values to the English currency or words terms that correspond to those values, as illustrated in the accompanying screenshot, you may do so. This section will discuss how to convert the numbers quickly and efficiently to their English equivalents.

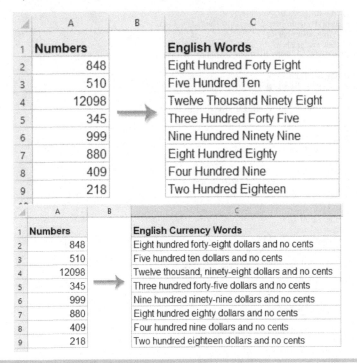

11.1 How to Convert the Number into Words?

Excel's built-in tools won't assist you in this instance, but you may use the program's User Defined Function to get the job done. Please follow these instructions:

If you push & hold your Alt key in conjunction with the F11 key, the Visual Basic für Applications window will open in your current window.

Then, paste the subsequent code into your Module Window and choose Insert ➔ Module.

```vba
Function NumberstoWords(ByVal MyNumber)
'Update by Extendoffice
Dim xStr As String
Dim xFNum As Integer
Dim xStrPoint
Dim xStrNumber
Dim xPoint As String
Dim xNumber As String
Dim xP() As Variant
Dim xDP
Dim xCnt As Integer
Dim xResult, xT As String
Dim xLen As Integer
On Error Resume Next
xP = Array("", "Thousand ", "Million ", "Billion ", "Trillion ", " ", " ", " ", " ")
xNumber = Trim(Str(MyNumber))
xDP = InStr(xNumber, ".")
xPoint = ""
xStrNumber = ""
If xDP > 0 Then
xPoint = " point "
xStr = Mid(xNumber, xDP + 1)
xStrPoint = Left(xStr, Len(xNumber) - xDP)
For xFNum = 1 To Len(xStrPoint)
xStr = Mid(xStrPoint, xFNum, 1)
xPoint = xPoint & GetDigits(xStr) & " "
Next xFNum
xNumber = Trim(Left(xNumber, xDP - 1))
End If
xCnt = 0
xResult = ""
xT = ""
xLen = 0
xLen = Int(Len(Str(xNumber)) / 3)
If (Len(Str(xNumber)) Mod 3) = 0 Then xLen = xLen - 1
Do While xNumber <> ""
If xLen = xCnt Then
xT = GetHundredsDigits(Right(xNumber, 3), False)
Else
If xCnt = 0 Then
xT = GetHundredsDigits(Right(xNumber, 3), True)
Else
xT = GetHundredsDigits(Right(xNumber, 3), False)
End If
End If
If xT <> "" Then
xResult = xT & xP(xCnt) & xResult
End If
If Len(xNumber) > 3 Then
xNumber = Left(xNumber, Len(xNumber) - 3)
Else
xNumber = ""
End If
xCnt = xCnt + 1
Loop
xResult = xResult & xPoint
NumberstoWords = xResult
End Function
Function GetHundredsDigits(xHDgt, xB As Boolean)
Dim xRStr As String
Dim xStrNum As String
Dim xStr As String
Dim xI As Integer
Dim xBB As Boolean
xStrNum = xHDgt
xRStr = ""
On Error Resume Next
xBB = True
If Val(xStrNum) = 0 Then Exit Function
xStrNum = Right("000" & xStrNum, 3)
xStr = Mid(xStrNum, 1, 1)
If xStr <> "0" Then
xRStr = GetDigits(Mid(xStrNum, 1, 1)) & "Hundred "
Else
If xB Then
xRStr = "and "
xBB = False
Else
xRStr = " "
xBB = False
```

```
End It
End If
If Mid(xStrNum, 2, 2) <> "oo" Then
xRStr = xRStr & GetTenDigits(Mid(xStrNum, 2, 2), xBB)
End If
GetHundredsDigits = xRStr
End Function
Function GetTenDigits(xTDgt, xB As Boolean)
Dim xStr As String
Dim xI As Integer
Dim xArr_1() As Variant
Dim xArr_2() As Variant
Dim xT As Boolean
xArr_1 = Array("Ten ", "Eleven ", "Twelve ", "Thirteen ", "Fourteen ", "Fifteen ", "Sixteen ", "Seve
xArr_2 = Array("", "", "Twenty ", "Thirty ", "Forty ", "Fifty ", "Sixty ", "Seventy ", "Eighty ", "Nine
xStr = ""
xT = True
On Error Resume Next
If Val(Left(xTDgt, 1)) = 1 Then
xI = Val(Right(xTDgt, 1))
If xB Then xStr = "and "
xStr = xStr & xArr_1(xI)
Else
xI = Val(Left(xTDgt, 1))
If Val(Left(xTDgt, 1)) > 1 Then
If xB Then xStr = "and "
xStr = xStr & xArr_2(Val(Left(xTDgt, 1)))
xT = False
End If
If xStr = "" Then
 If xB Then
 xStr = "and "
 End If
End If
If Right(xTDgt, 1) <> "o" Then
xStr = xStr & GetDigits(Right(xTDgt, 1))
End If
End If
GetTenDigits = xStr
End Function
Function GetDigits(xDgt)
Dim xStr As String
Dim xArr_1() As Variant
xArr_1 = Array("Zero ", "One ", "Two ", "Three ", "Four ", "Five ", "Six ", "Seven ", "Eight ", "Nine
xStr = ""
On Error Resume Next
xStr = xArr_1(Val(xDgt))
GetDigits = xStr
End Function
```

3. Save & exit this code, then return to the worksheet and insert the formula =NumberstoWords(A2) into a blank cell (where A2 is the cell containing the number you wish to convert to an English word; see screenshot for reference).

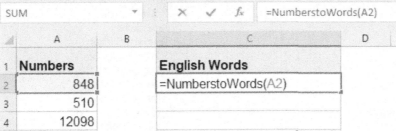

After that, you'd enter the formula in cell C2, hit the enter key, and then move your fill handle to a range you wish to include. Each numerical value has been translated into its English equivalent.

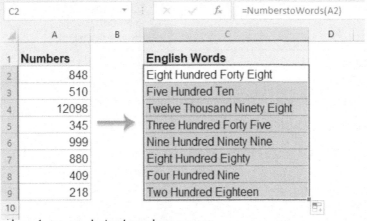

This code supports integer numbers; however, decimal numbers are not.

Convert Numbers to Currency Words with User-Defined Function
Use the following VBA code to transform the numbers into their English currency names.
If you press & hold your Alt key in conjunction with the F11 key, the Visual Basic for Application window will open in your current window.
Then, in the Module Window, paste your following code and choose Insert > Module.

```
Function SpellNumberToEnglish(ByVal pNumber)
'Update by Extendoffice
Dim Dollars, Cents
arr = Array("", "", " Thousand ", " Million ", " Billion ", " Trillion ")
pNumber = Trim(Str(pNumber))
xDecimal = InStr(pNumber, ".")
If xDecimal > 0 Then
    Cents = GetTens(Left(Mid(pNumber, xDecimal + 1) & "00", 2))
    pNumber = Trim(Left(pNumber, xDecimal - 1))
End If
xIndex = 1
Do While pNumber <> ""
    xHundred = ""
    xValue = Right(pNumber, 3)
    If Val(xValue) <> 0 Then
        xValue = Right("000" & xValue, 3)
        If Mid(xValue, 1, 1) <> "0" Then
            xHundred = GetDigit(Mid(xValue, 1, 1)) & " Hundred "
        End If
        If Mid(xValue, 2, 1) <> "0" Then
            xHundred = xHundred & GetTens(Mid(xValue, 2))
        Else
            xHundred = xHundred & GetDigit(Mid(xValue, 3))
        End If
    End If
    If xHundred <> "" Then
        Dollars = xHundred & arr(xIndex) & Dollars
    End If
    If Len(pNumber) > 3 Then
        pNumber = Left(pNumber, Len(pNumber) - 3)
    Else
        pNumber = ""
    End If
    xIndex = xIndex + 1
Loop
Select Case Dollars
    Case ""
        Dollars = "No Dollars"
    Case "One"
        Dollars = "One Dollar"
    Case Else
        Dollars = Dollars & " Dollars"
End Select
Select Case Cents
    Case ""
        Cents = " and No Cents"
    Case "One"
        Cents = " and One Cent"
    Case Else
        Cents = " and " & Cents & " Cents"
End Select
SpellNumberToEnglish = Dollars & Cents
End Function
Function GetTens(pTens)
Dim Result As String
Result = ""
If Val(Left(pTens, 1)) = 1 Then
    Select Case Val(pTens)
        Case 10: Result = "Ten"
        Case 11: Result = "Eleven"
        Case 12: Result = "Twelve"
        Case 13: Result = "Thirteen"
        Case 14: Result = "Fourteen"
        Case 15: Result = "Fifteen"
        Case 16: Result = "Sixteen"
        Case 17: Result = "Seventeen"
        Case 18: Result = "Eighteen"
        Case 19: Result = "Nineteen"
        Case Else
    End Select
Else
    Select Case Val(Left(pTens, 1))
        Case 2: Result = "Twenty "
        Case 3: Result = "Thirty "
        Case 4: Result = "Forty "
        Case 5: Result = "Fifty "
        Case 6: Result = "Sixty "
        Case 7: Result = "Seventy "
        Case 8: Result = "Eighty "
        Case 9: Result = "Ninety "
        Case Else
    End Select
    Result = Result & GetDigit(Right(pTens, 1))
End If
GetTens = Result
End Function
Function GetDigit(pDigit)
Select Case Val(pDigit)
    Case 1: GetDigit = "One"
    Case 2: GetDigit = "Two"
    Case 3: GetDigit = "Three"
    Case 4: GetDigit = "Four"
    Case 5: GetDigit = "Five"
    Case 6: GetDigit = "Six"
    Case 7: GetDigit = "Seven"
    Case 8: GetDigit = "Eight"
    Case 9: GetDigit = "Nine"
    Case Else: GetDigit = ""
End Select
End Function
```

3. Return to the worksheet, enter the formula =SpellNumberToEnglish(A2) (where A2 is the cell containing the number to be converted to an English currency word), and drag your fill handle downwards to the cells to which you want to apply this formula; the numbers have been spelled out into English currency words.

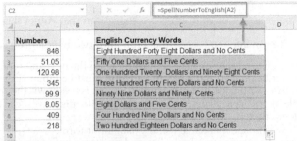

Convert Numbers to Currency Words with A Useful Feature

Since the formula can be challenging for Excel rookies to decipher, here you will learn a helpful tool: Kutools for your Excel's Numbers to Words.

Tips:

Download Kutools for Excel to use the Numbers towards Words feature and afterward apply the feature in a flash.

Please follow these steps once Kutools for Excel has been installed:

To do this, first, choose the numbers you need to convert, then go to Kutools ➔ Content ➔ Numbers-Words (see screenshot)

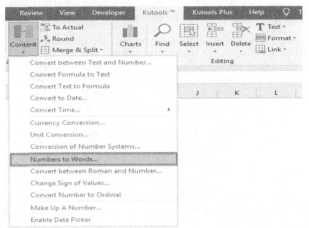

After clicking the Ok button within the Numbers-Currency Phrases dialogue box, you'll notice that the numbers are being converted into their English currency names.

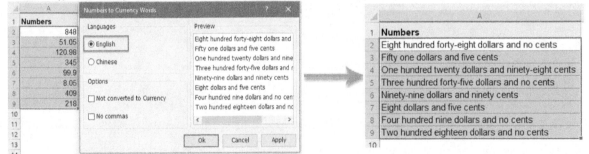

Hint: In the Options menu, choose the Not transformed to Currency tick box if you'd want to view the original English.

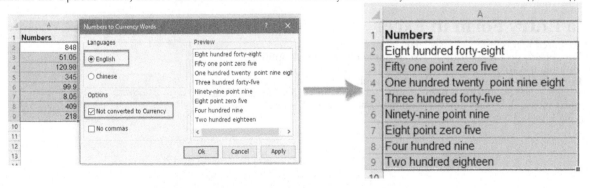

Chapter 12: Excel Data Entry Form

If you need to enter data, Excel offers several functions that will come in handy. This data entry form is one such function.

In this chapter, you will discover about data input forms & how to make and utilize them in Excel.

Why It's Important to Understand Data Entry Forms?

You do not!

Nonetheless, if the data input is a regular aspect of your job, it's a suggestion that you evaluate out this function to see how much time it might save you.

When entering data into Excel, you have run into (and seen others run into) two typical problems:

- It's time-consuming. After finishing with one cell, you must go on to the next and repeat the process. You may need to scroll up to determine what column it belongs to and what information must be input. If there are a number of columns, you may either scroll to the right and afterward back to the beginning or just scroll down the page.
- It's error-prone. For example, if you have a large data set requiring 40 entries, you can accidentally type something into a cell that wasn't meant to be entered there.

The procedure may be sped up and made more dependable using a data input form.

Let's demonstrate briefly what an Excel data input form looks like and performs before demonstrating how to make one.

Listed below is a collection of information that a company's human resources department normally keeps.

	A	B	C	D	E
1	Date	Name	Area	Interviewed By	Status
2	01-08-2018	Mike Banes	Admin	John Lopez	Rejected
3	03-08-2018	Ross Taylor	PHP	David Peters	Hired
4	07-08-2018	Steve Grant	PHP	Helen Bash	In-progress
5	08-08-2018	Ruth Fowler	Java	Carolyn Johnson	In-progress

Each time a new record must be added, the user will have to choose a cell within the next available row, then enter the necessary information for each column, one at a time.

This method works OK; however, using an Excel data entry form would save time and effort.

A data input form for this dataset is provided below for your convenience.

You should input your information in the marked areas. When you are through adding information, press Enter to add it to the table and continue onto the next row.

Here's a sample of how it operates:

There is just one dialogue box to complete, making this far simpler than standard data entering.

12.1 Data Entry Form in Excel

Preparation is required before using an Excel data input form.

If you've tried to utilize a data input form in Excel, you know it's not an option.

The first step in using it is to drag its icon onto your Quick Access Toolbar.

Including a Form for Data Entry in the Quick Launch Menu

Here's how to make a data input form a permanent fixture on your Quick Launch Menu:

To use the context menu, right-click anywhere on the Quick Access Toolbar.

Select "Set Up My Quick Access Toolbar."

When the "Excel Options" window appears, choose the "All Commands" menu item.

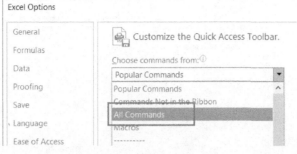

Select "Form" from the drop-down menu of options.

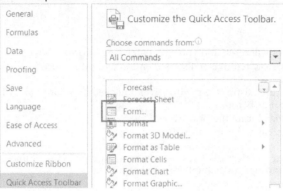

To include, choose the "Add" option.

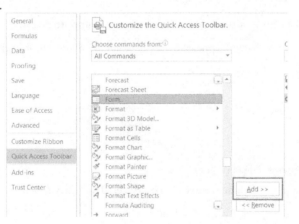

Proceed with the OK button.

Following the instructions above, you'll find the Form icon in your QAT (as shown below).

When ready to make the entry, open the QAT file, click the Form icon, and choose the cell in the dataset where you wish to make the change.

Data must be in your Excel Table to function properly for the Data Entry Form. Unless it already is, you'll need to format it as a table in Excel (Control + T).

12.2 Parts of the Data Entry Form

Excel's built-in data entry form is replete with options (as you may see below).

Follow on for a brief rundown of what all buttons do:

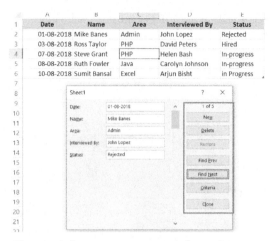

- **New:** If you do this, the form will reset, and you may enter new information.
- **Delete:** As a result, you may now remove an existing entry. When I choose Mike Banes and then press the Delete key, his information will be removed.
- **Restore:** If you are updating an existing entry and haven't clicked New or pushed Enter, the form will revert to its former state, allowing you to update it as before.
- **Find Prev:** Using this, you may locate the prior record.
- **Find Next:** The next record will be located using this.
- **Criteria:** The ability to locate certain documents is therefore granted. To locate all the entries in which the candidate's Status is Hired, you would first need to select the Criteria button, then type "Hired" into the Status box, and then utilize the find buttons. This lesson will go through an example of this later.
- **Close:** Doing so will end the form.
- **Scroll Bar:** To see further data, utilize the scroll bar.

Let's look at all the possibilities of an Excel Data Entry form now.
Remember that you can't use the Data Entry form dialogue box until you've imported your data into your Excel table & then selected a column in the table.
To the right is an example of the prompt that will appear if you try to act like Excel without first selecting a cell:

12.3 Creating Another New Entry

The following are the actions required to add a new entry to your Excel Data Entry Form:
To begin, choose a cell inside the Excel Table.
To access the Form, choose it from the Quick Access Toolbar.

Complete your form by putting the required information.
If you choose to add a new record to the table, you may do so by pressing the Enter key (or clicking the new button).

12.4 Navigating Through the Existing Records

Data Entry Form allows you to move around quickly and change your data without exiting the dialogue window.
This may be extremely helpful if you're working with a dataset with several columns. Using this method, you can avoid having to repeatedly scroll and click back and forth.
Here's how to use a data input form to go around and amend the files:
To begin, choose a cell in Excel Table.
To access the Form, choose it from Quick Access Toolbar.
You may use the 'Find Next' & 'Find Prev' buttons to navigate to the next & previous entries, respectively.

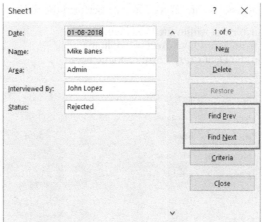

Make your modifications & press enter to save them. If you mistake entering data and later decide you want to go back to the original version, you could do so by ticking the "Restore" button.

If you'd rather see the results one by one, use the scroll bar.

In the subsequent screenshot, you can find out how simple navigation works in action by scrolling over a set of data.

Alternatively, you may use filters to swiftly sift through all the data.

For all entries where the status is "In-progress," for instance, you may perform the following:

- Make your selection in any available cell within the Excel table.
- To access the Form, choose it from your Quick Access Toolbar.
- Select the Criteria option within the Data Entry Form dialogue box.

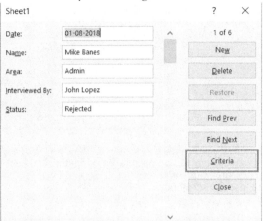

Type "In Progress" into the Status column. This is a case-insensitive value. This means that IN-PROGRESS may be used instead.

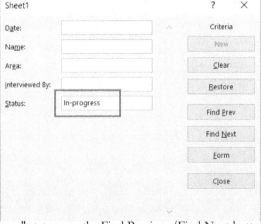

To see the items with a current "In Progress" status, use the Find Previous/Find Next buttons.
The criterion function is invaluable when searching through a large dataset for records that fit certain criteria.
Keep in mind that you may search the database using a combination of several criterion fields.
To examine only entries with the status "In-progress" that were created on or after August 7, 2018, you may set the date filter to ">07-08-2018" and the status filter to "In-progress." When using Find Previous/Find Next, entries with the status In-progress created on or after 07-08-2018 will now be shown.

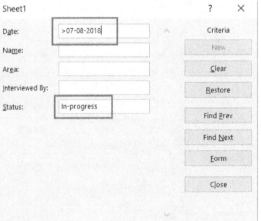

Criteria may also make use of wildcard characters.
For instance, you may need wildcard characters to retrieve entries when the same information has been entered with different spellings of the same term (such as in process, in progress, in-progress, and InProgress).
Here are the measures to take:

- Make your selection in any available cell within your Excel table.
- To access the Form, choose it from a Quick Access Toolbar.

- To use, choose the Criteria tab.
- Type *progress into the Status box.

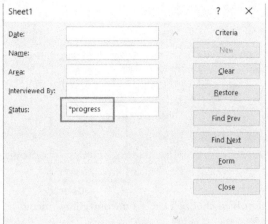

To see the items with a current "In Progress" status, use the Find Previous/Find Next buttons.
The asterisk (*) serves as a "wildcard" character that may stand in for any other characters in Excel. So, if the status says "progress," the Find Previous and Find Next buttons will find it no matter where it comes in the list.

12.5 Deleting a Record

Records may be removed directly from your Data Entry form.
This is helpful if you want to search for a certain category of data to remove them.
Using Data Entry Form, a record may be deleted as detailed below:

- Make your selection in any available cell within the Excel table.
- To access the Form, choose it from your Quick Access Toolbar.
- Find the specific entry you want to remove and click it.
- Just hit the delete button.

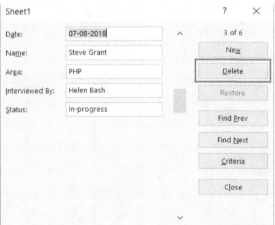

It may seem like a huge amount of effort only to input and browse information, but if you're working with a big data and entering data often, you'll appreciate the time savings.

12.6 Restricting Data Entry Based on Rules

Data validation within cells may be used to check that information entered meets certain criteria.
For instance, the data validation rule may be set up to restrict the data input field to just dates.
A user will be presented with an error if they try to input information that isn't a date.
To make these regulations while inputting data, follow these steps:

- The data validation rule may be applied to a range of cells or an entire column. Here you've chosen to focus on the first column, A.
- To get the information, use the "Data" menu.

Gil B. Dreher

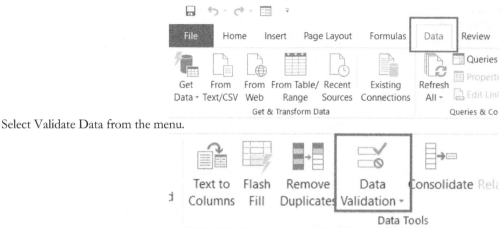

Select Validate Data from the menu.

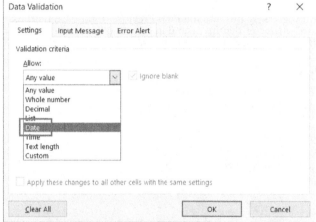

On your 'Settings' tab of a 'Data Validation' box, choose 'Date' from your 'Allow' menu.

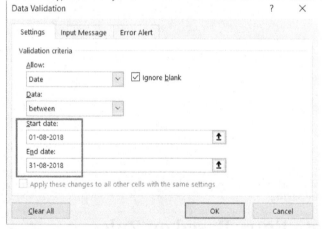

Please include both a beginning and an ending date. Only submissions made between these dates will be considered.

Proceed with the OK button.

It is now forbidden to insert anything other than dates into the Date field of the data entry form.

A notification like this will appear before your eyes:

Also, data validation may be used in conjunction with data input forms to prevent users from accidentally providing inaccurate information. It may be helpful when dealing with numerical data, textual length, dates, etc.

Some tips and tricks for using the Xls Data Entry Form are as follows:

You may search the data using wildcards (through the criteria option).

For Data Entry Form to work, you'll need an Excel table. Another requirement for submitting the form is to choose a cell inside it. With one notable exception, though. The Excel Form would still refer to the named range you provide in the Form's Data Source even if you possess an Excel table.

When filling out the Data Entry form, the width of the fields will change based on the width of the data columns. The same will be reflected within the form if the column width is too small.

The data input form supports the use of bullet points. Use your keyboard's numeric keypad shortcuts ALT + 7 or ALT + 9.

12.7 How to Use the Data Validation Along with the Data Entry Form?

Choose the cells that will be affected by the new rule.

Pick out Data ➔ Data Validation.

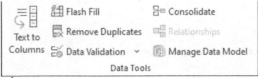

Under Allow under Settings, choose a mode:

- Whole Number - put a cap on the cell's input to only take whole numbers.
- Decimal - limit the cell's numeric input to decimal places only.
- List - to choose information from a pull-down menu.
- Date - So that only dates may be entered into the cell.
- Time - such that only time may enter the cell.
- Text Length - for the sake of keeping the text brief.
- Custom – concerning individualized formulas.

Go to Data and choose a criterion.

Based on your selections in the Allow and Data fields, fill in the remaining mandatory fields.

The Input Message option allows you to create a personalized message that will appear to users when they input information.

If you need the message to display when the user picks or hovers over the chosen cell, click the Display input message once a cell is chosen checkbox (s).

Navigate to the Error Alert menu item to tweak the error message & choose a formatting option.

Click the OK button.

When the user put in some invalid value, the Error Alert displays the message you specify.

12.8 How to Open the Data Entry Form With VBA?

The names, phone numbers, ages, and sexes of certain clients at these three bank locations are included in separate spreadsheets labeled New York, Washington, and California.

Customer Name	Contact Address	Age	Gender
Morris Johnson	444418198	23	Male
Steve Smith	444658817	22	Male
Richard Hadley	444812454	35	Male
Usman Khaja	444878614	44	Male
Isha Guja	444795695	65	Female
Angela Hopkins	444105773	43	Female
Craig Arvin	444918322	61	Male
Ricky Austin	444998259	67	Male
Ijack Simpson	444771430	25	Male
Marcus North	444967054	35	Male
Frank Orwell	444630462	28	Male

Today, you'll use VBA to design a form for entering information into the database.

You have a two-stage plan to reach your goal.

To begin, a UserForm for inputting data will be developed; once complete, a button will be added to the relevant worksheets for easy access.

In the first stage, you'll use Excel VBA to design a UserForm that will serve as the data entry form.

This is a lengthy procedure, and it may take a while before you grasp it. Therefore, do the actions listed below as precisely and patiently as possible for an efficient result.

Use the ALT + F11 keys on your keyboard to bring up Visual Basic.

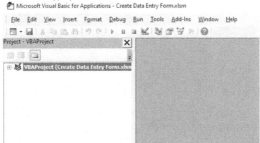

Select Insert ➔ UserForm from the Visual Basic menu bar. Go ahead and choose UserForm. UserForm1 will launch as a new UserForm.

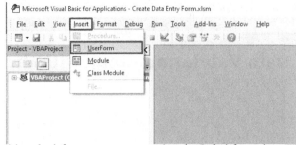

First, bring up the UserForm and position the leftmost top corner using the Label from the toolbox. Put Worksheet in place of Label as the title.

Put a list box to the right of Label1.

Then, to the left of the UserForm, drag as many Labels as there are data columns (four in this case). Put a TextBox next to each Label. Set the Labels to show the names of your data columns (Customer Name, Age, Contact Address, & Gender here).

After that, position a CommandButton on the UserForm's right-most bottom edge. Simply renaming the button "Enter Data" will do the trick.

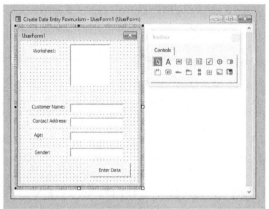

Start by doubling-clicking the Listbox. When you click ListBox1, a hidden subroutine named ListBox1 Click will launch. Simply type in the following security code.

VBA Code:

Private Sub **ListBox1_Click**()

For **i** = 0 To **UserForm1**.**ListBox1**.ListCount - 1
  If **UserForm1**.**ListBox1**.Selected(**i**) = True Then
    Worksheets(**UserForm1**.**ListBox1**.List(**i**)).Activate
  End If
Next **i**

End Sub
Copy

```
Private Sub ListBox1_Click()

For i = 0 To UserForm1.ListBox1.ListCount - 1
    If UserForm1.ListBox1.Selected(i) = True Then
        Worksheets(UserForm1.ListBox1.List(i)).Activate
    End If
Next i

End Sub
```

In the next step, double-click the CommandButton. A separate, hidden sub procedure named CommandButton Click will launch if you click the Command button. Type in the following security code.

```
Private Sub CommandButton1_Click()

Total_Rows = ActiveSheet.UsedRange.Rows.Count
Total_Columns = ActiveSheet.UsedRange.Columns.Count

Active_Column = 1

For Each Ctrl In UserForm1.Controls
    If TypeName(Ctrl) = "TextBox" Then
        ActiveSheet.UsedRange.Cells(Total_Rows + 1, Active_Column) = Ctrl.Text
        Active_Column = Active_Column + 1
    End If
Next Ctrl

End Sub
```

At last, choose Module from the Insert submenu of the toolbar.

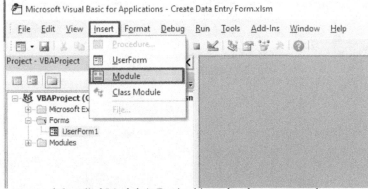

As a replacement, you'll add a new module called Module1. Put in this code when prompted:

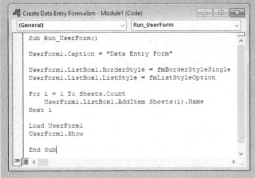

That's it; you're finished. New information may now be added to the database using the data input form you just constructed.

Second, you'll create a button that will launch the data entry screen

Congratulations, you have completed the data input form using an Excel VBA Userform. Your forms will be accessible through a new button that you will add to your worksheets.

To do this, do what is outlined below.

Select the Developer tab on Excel's Ribbon at the top and click it to open it. By default, Excel's Developer tab is hidden. If it's hidden from the Excel Ribbon and you want to view it, do what you've instructed.

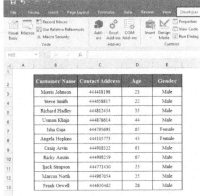

Select Controls and then click Insert under the Developer tab. Several useful tools are at your disposal. You may move a button (form command) from the upper left.

Gil B. Dreher

The worksheet area where you want to place the button may be resized by dragging and dropping it there. The Assign Macro dialogue box will pop up. Just type "Run UserForm" into the Macro name box.

Then choose the OK button.
You may customize the button's appearance at this time. Please enter new information; you updated it.

Congratulations! You just created a button to access the data entering screen.
Your worksheets may be made more complex by adding a button if desired.
Third, use the completed form as a data-entry template.
With the help of Excel VBA, you could create a button that opens a data input form. Click the worksheet "Enter New Data" button to see the results.
An input form will pop up for you to fill out. To begin, go to the worksheet menu and choose the one where you wish to enter the data.
As an example, you'll choose New York. When you choose a certain sheet, it will start to be used.

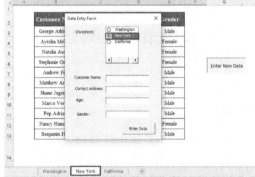

The remaining fields may then be completed with the necessary information. You've entered 444204240, Jennifer Marlo, 26 years old, female.

Following that, choose the "Enter Data" option.
The updated information may be found in the very last database record.

Chapter 13: Excel Valuation Modeling

In this chapter, you will go through Excel Valuation Modeling and different methods of valuation modeling.

13.1 Valuation Modeling

Numerous approaches to determining a company's worth may be modeled in Excel; they include discounted cash flow (DCF) analysis, similar precedent transactions, trading multiples, and ratios like the horizontal and vertical analysis. These Excel analyses may be created from scratch or based on an existing template/model. Many different types of financial experts often engage in this kind of employment.

13.2 Why Perform Valuation Modeling in Excel?

Professionals in various fields devote considerable effort to valuation modeling in Excel due to its usefulness in various contexts. Just a few examples of why:

- Getting ready to seek funding from investors (determining what cost shares must be issued at)
- The process of selling a company and determining an acceptable price range.
- Acquiring a business and determining a fair purchase price
- For providing stock to workers (an ESOP or Employee Ownership Plan)
- For use in house budgeting and planning
- Business succession preparation
- Assess investments for major construction projects.
- Analyses of Impairment (related to every significant reduction in asset values)
- Insolvency and other legal processes

13.3 How to Execute Excel Valuation Modeling?

As was said, 3 major ways to determine a company's worth exist. The most thorough way, often the most relied upon, is the discounted cash flows, or DCFs, analysis. How to conduct each modeling technique is detailed below.

Discounted cash flows modeling into Excel

To use the DCF method, a finance expert must collect financial data from the previous three to five years for the company in question and enter it into the Excel model. The next step is establishing a dynamic connection between the three financial statements.

After that, projections are created using Excel formulae based on the assumptions established about the company's future performance (typically, about 5 years into your future). Finally, they derive the company's terminal value by discounting the projected period & the terminal value back into the present using the average weighted capital cost (WACC).

Comparable trading multiple into Excel

Excel's similar multiples valuation approach is different compared to a DCF model. Instead of relying on the firm's intrinsic value (as in the first technique), an analyst might use the valuation multiple of similar publicly listed businesses to estimate the worth of the company or companies in question. Common valuation multiples include Price/Book, Price/Earnings, Price/Revenue, and Price/EBITDA.

Company Name	Price ($/share)	Shares (M)	Market Cap ($M)	Net Debt	EV ($M)	Sales ($M)	EBITDA ($M)	Earnings ($M)	EV/Sales x	EV/EBITDA x	P/E x
Micro Partners	$9.45	100	$945	$125	$1,070	$268	$76	$47	4.0x	14.1x	20.1x
Junior Enterprises	$5.68	1,250	$7,100	$2,000	$9,100	$4,136	$778	$412	2.2x	11.7x	17.2x
Miniature Company	$18.11	50	$906	$25	$931	$443	$96	$56	2.1x	9.7x	16.3x
Average Limited	$12.27	630	$7,730	$350	$8,080	$1,949	$528	$294	4.1x	15.3x	26.3x
Bohemeth Industires	$9.03	1,500	$13,545	$0	$13,545	$6,622	$795	$423	2.0x	17.0x	32.0x
Average									2.9x	13.6x	22.4x
Median									2.2x	14.1x	20.1x

Precedent transactions modeling in Excel

The third method of Excel value modeling involves researching the prices at which comparable firms were acquired in the past. Like similar trading multiples, this is a relative valuation method,
but it considers the value of control (the takeover premium) and uses historical transactions (which may quickly be out of date).

Date	Target	Transaction Value ($M)	Buyers	Sales	EBITDA	EBIT	EV/Sales	EV/EBITDA	EV/EBIT
01-24-2018	Current Ltd	2,350	Average Limited	1,237			1.9x	na	na
04-19-2016	Recent Inc	6,500	Bohemeth Industires	4,643	808	515	1.4x	8.0x	12.6x
04-19-2014	Past Co	2,150	Other Group	1,693	249	178	1.3x	8.7x	12.1x
11-07-2014	Historical LLP	450	Junior Enterprises	197			2.3x	na	na
11-01-2012	Old Group	325	Minature Company	64	17	15	5.1x	18.8x	21.5x
10-07-2011	Dated Enterprises	150	Micro Partners	71	16		2.1x	9.3x	na
Average							2.3x	11.2x	15.4x
Median							2.0x	9.0x	12.6x

13.4 Jobs That Perform Valuation Modeling in Excel

It takes years of school and experience for financial experts to acquire the various specialized abilities necessary to make these evaluations.

- Accounting is one of the most crucial abilities to have (financial statements, principles, methods)
- Finance (formulas, financial math, ratios, calculations)
- Excel (Excel shortcuts, best practices, functions)
- Strategy (market analysis, competitive advantage)
- Valuation (a grouping of all preceding skills)

Unlike some other qualifications, CFI's Financial Analyst Certifications cover all of them in a single comprehensive online course.
Valuation modeling in Excel-based jobs
Using Excel to learn how to calculate the worth of a business, division, or investment opportunity is a valuable ability that can be used in various professional settings.
The following are just a few examples of popular professions that call on certain abilities:
Funding banking (associate and analyst level)
Equity Investments & Startup Funding (associate and analyst level)
Business expansion (manager and analyst level)
The Analysis and Planning of Finances (director, manager, analyst level)
Financial reporting to the public (impairment testing, transaction advisory)
Investing Study (analyst and associate level)

13.5 Main Valuation Methods

Depending on your perspective, Excel's versatility may be used for good or ill. When it comes to financial modeling, even though bigger companies may try to utilize software, Excel is usually what they wind up using in the end.

The most common justifications for using Excel are as follows:

- Complete adaptability and personalization
- Extremely cheap to buy
- Simple to disseminate to a wider audience
- Universally accessible and comprehensible No "black box" complexity; straightforward implementation and audibility

However, Excel's extensive customization options also increase the risk of mistakes, erroneous calculations, and sloppy procedures creeping into models. Analysts and other financial professionals should make it a priority to master Excel modeling and fully comprehend prevalent industry standards.

Chapter 14: Mathematical and Statistical Functions

In this chapter, you will go through advanced excel functions utilized into corporate word including Mathematical function and statistical function.

14.1 Excel Math Functions

Math functions are used to conduct numerical operations such as adding, doing rudimentary financial analysis, and calculating percentages of totals.

Sum Function

You may use the SUM function in Excel to add up or total the values of many rows or columns.

=SUM (num 1, [num 2])

To make advantage of the SUM function

Build the SUM functionality inside the cell.

Head to the Function argument if you want to choose cells for the cell range box.

In addition to this, hit the Enter key.

The SUM function requires the following parameters to work properly.

=SUM (number1, [number2], [number3]......)

- **Number1(Required Argument)**: This is the first value to sum
- **Number2 (Optional Argument)**: This is the second value to sum
- **Number3 (Optional Argument)**: This is the third value to sum

Let's utilize the Aggregate function in the table to determine how much money was made from Monday through Friday.

	A	B	C
1	DAYS OF THE WEEK	SALES	
2	MONDAY	23,000	
3	TUESDAY	12,990	
4	WEDNESDAY	12,987	
5	THURSAY	32,200	
6	FRIDAY	32,150	

To calculate the revenue for the five business days, Monday through Friday, using Total, follow the methods below.

Complete the feature by setting the cell in an empty cell to be summarized using the =SUM formula (A2:B6)

	A	B	C	D	E	F
1	DAYS OF THE WEEK	SALES				
2	MONDAY	23,000				
3	TUESDAY	12,990				
4	WEDNESDAY	12,987				
5	THURSAY	32,200				
6	FRIDAY	32,150				
7						
8	TOTAL SALES	=SUM(A2:B6)				
9		SUM(number1, [number2], ...)				

If you satisfied the above standards, your net revenue from Monday through Friday would be 1,133.27.

	A	B	C	D	E	F
1	DAYS OF THE WEEK	SALES				
2	MONDAY	23,000				
3	TUESDAY	12,990				
4	WEDNESDAY	12,987				
5	THURSAY	32,200				
6	FRIDAY	32,150				
7						
8	TOTAL SALES	113327				

Take this into mind when working with the SUM function.

A value error would occur if the criteria supplied are more than 255 characters in length.

When using the SUM technique, empty cell types that contain text values are immediately disqualified.

As parameters, you may use everything from constants and sets to named ranges and cell references.

Every statement that contains mistakes will result in an error being returned by the SUM function.

SUMIF Function

When given a collection of parameters or conditions, the SUM function totals the contents of each cell.

Made available, Dates and statistics, as well as texts, are used to formulate the criteria or standards.

In addition, logical operators such as and > as well as wildcards (* and?) are used in this work.

The SUMIF method makes use of the following parameters in its computations.

=SUMIF (range, criteria, [sum_range]

The range of cells against which the criteria are extended is referred to as the range in the mandatory argument.

The mandatory argument for the criterion is that it determines which cells may be joined together. There are many ways that justifications for criteria might be presented.

Values such as a number, an integer, or the passage of time are all instances of numerical values.

Text strings include instances such as Monday, East, Price, and so on.

Examples of the terms "above 11" and "under 3."

The sum range is an optional argument that may be used. This cell should be used to total any additional cells that need to be added to the ones specified in the range argument.

The implementation of SUMIF

Let's check whether the SUMIF function is being utilized by calculating the revenue in January in the United States and January in the United States.

	A	B	C	D
		B10		
1	MONTH	COUNTRY	SALES	
2	JAN	USA	23,000	
3	FEB	ENGLAND	12,990	
4	JAN	USA	12,987	
5	MARCH	FRANCE	32,200	
6	JAN	ITALY	32,150	
7	FEB	USA	33,212	
8	JAN	USA	12,900	

To begin, you will need to determine how much money you earned in January using one of the techniques provided below.

Complete the task by replacing the already configured cell to round up with a blank cell. SUM (A 2: A 8

SEARCH =SUMIF(A2:A8

	A	B	C	D	E
1	MONTH	COUNTRY	SALES		
2	JAN	USA	23,000		
3	FEB	ENGLAND	12,990		
4	JAN	USA	12,987		
5	MARCH	FRANCE	32,200		
6	JAN	ITALY	32,150		
7	FEB	USA	33,212		
8	JAN	USA	12,900		
9	TOTAL SALES FOR JAN	=SUMIF(A2:A8			
10		SUMIF(range, criteria, [sum_range])			

Complete the necessary fields for the January SUM (A 2: A 8, "JAN", "")

SEARCH =SUMIF(A2:A8, "JAN")

	A	B	C	D	E	F
1	MONTH	COUNTRY	SALES			
2	JAN	USA	23,000			
3	FEB	ENGLAND	12,990			
4	JAN	USA	12,987			
5	MARCH	FRANCE	32,200			
6	JAN	ITALY	32,150			
7	FEB	USA	33,212			
8	JAN	USA	12,900			
9	TOTAL SALES FOR JAN	=SUMIF(A2:A8, "JAN")				
10		SUMIF(range, criteria, [sum_range])				

Then put in the sum_range; **SUM (A2:A8, "JAN", C2;C8)**

SEARCH		× ✓ *fx*	=SUMIF(A2:A8, "JAN",C2:C8)		

	A	B	C	D	E	F	G
1	MONTH	COUNTRY	SALES				
2	JAN	USA	23,000				
3	FEB	ENGLAND	12,990				
4	JAN	USA	12,987				
5	MARCH	FRANCE	32,200				
6	JAN	ITALY	32,150				
7	FEB	USA	33,212				
8	JAN	USA	12,900				
9	TOTAL SALES FOR JAN	=SUMIF(A2:A8, "JAN",C2:C8)					

As can be seen in the table that follows, there were a total of 81,037 sales for January.

B9		× ✓ *fx*	=SUMIF(A2:A8, "JAN",C2:C8)		

	A	B	C	D	E	F	G
1	MONTH	COUNTRY	SALES				
2	JAN	USA	23,000				
3	FEB	ENGLAND	12,990				
4	JAN	USA	12,987				
5	MARCH	FRANCE	32,200				
6	JAN	ITALY	32,150				
7	FEB	USA	33,212				
8	JAN	USA	12,900				
9	TOTAL SALES FOR JAN	81,037					

Calculate the total amount of money earned through sales in the USA.
Fill in the blank cell corresponding to the role played by the cell set that will be summed up using the formula =SUM (B 2: B 8.

SEARCH		× ✓ *fx*	=SUMIF(B2:B8,	

	A	B	C	D	E
1	MONTH	COUNTRY	SALES		
2	JAN	USA	23,000		
3	FEB	ENGLAND	12,990		
4	JAN	USA	12,987		
5	MARCH	FRANCE	32,200		
6	JAN	ITALY	32,150		
7	FEB	USA	33,212		
8	JAN	USA	12,900		
9	TOTAL SALES FOR JAN	81,037			
10	TOTAL SALES MADE IN USA	=SUMIF(B2:B8,			
11		SUMIF(range, **criteria**, [sum_range])			

Put in the criteria which are **USA; SUM(B2:B8 "USA"**

Then put in the sum_range; **SUM(B2:B8, "USA", B2:B8)**

The total amount of money earned through sales in the United States is shown in the following table.

Take this into mind when you are working with the SUMIF FUNCTION.

An instance of the VALUE! Error occurs if the user supplies criteria that are longer than 255 characters.

Since the sum range has not been specified, the cells that fall inside that range will automatically be added up.

If you don't enclose text strings in parameters with double quotes, the content won't be able to fit.

Where do the wildcards come into play in the SUMIF function? And the asterisk may be utilized.

The Role of SUMIFs

The SUMIFS function may aggregate cells into a single output when those cells meet several criteria or conditions. The criteria or the requirements may be crafted using a combination of text, numbers, and times. This function uses logical operators like>, and so on, in addition to wildcards like * and?

Utilization of SUMIFS

Let's begin by calculating the overall number of apples that Pete has given you using the SUMIFS function and the table provided below.

Just follow the instructions outlined below to get the total quantity of apples that Pete contributed.

Fill up the section that contains the cell that has been configured to be added up = SUMIFS(C2: C 6, A2: A 6, "apples", B 2: B 6, "Pete") with a blank cell.

If the procedure is followed exactly, the total apples that have been provided will amount to 180.

Maintain compliance with the following requirements when utilizing the SUMIFS elements:

- For a standard, text string need to be enclosed in double quotation marks (ʻ), such as "orange.
- The sum range's column and row counts need to be the same as those of the extra range.
- A #VALUE error occurs if the given ranges are not in alignment with one another.
- Cell references aren't included in quotation marks anywhere in the standards.
- SUMIFS should never be used on arrays and only applied on ranges.

MOD Function

The MOD function is used to get the residual left over after a dividend, which is a sum divided by another integer (divisor).

The MOD function receives the parameters that have been presented so far:

(Required assumption) You need to get the remainder for that number; thus, that's the one you need to look up (Mandatory Argument)
Divisor: The number by which you want to divide the total amount.
Functional Application of the MOD Symbol
Find the remaining cell in the table that follows that is labeled A2 by making use of the MOD function.

	A	B	C	D
1	Number	Divisor	MOD FUNCTION	
2	23	2		
3	21	3		
4				
5				
6				

Identify the location of A2 by doing the following actions:
Insert the function that will be used, the numbers, and the divisor into the cell that is now empty by typing =MOD (A2, B2).

=MOD(A2, B2)

	A	B	C	D
1	Number	Divisor	MOD FUNCTION	
2	23	2	=MOD(A2, B2)	
3	21	3	MOD(number, divisor)	
4				
5				

The results of the prior maneuver are shown in the figure that can be seen below.

=MOD(A2, B2)

	A	B	C
1	Number	Divisor	MOD FUNCTION
2	23	2	1
3	21	3	

Keep the following when working with the MOD function in mind: #DID/0! An error is produced if the divisor's value is negative. If you used the MOD function, the result would have the same sign as the divisor.

Round Function
It has been decided to define the ROUND function, which will raise the total number of digits in a number. This function offers users the choice of rounding either up or down. The ROUND function will make use of the parameters that came before it.
Number1 (Required Argument): This is the number you want to be rounded up to the closest whole number.
Num digits are the number of digits that should be rounded before it is used. This argument is required.
Using the ROUND Function in Excel
The value 1844.123 should be rounded using the Circular function to one decimal point, two decimal places, the closest number, the nearer 10, the nearer 100, and the nearer 1000.
Round the number 1844.123 to the closest decimal point using the formula: (A1,1)

=ROUND(A1,1)

	A	B	C
1	1844.123	1844.1	
2			

Round to the closest integer by inputting 1844.123 and using the =ROUND function (A1, 0)

ROUNDDOWN Function
You may round integers down from a predetermined set of decimal places with the assistance of the ROUND DOWN tool.
The ROUND DOWN function makes advantage of the parameters that have come before it.
=ROUNDUP (number, num_digits)
Number1 (Required Argument): This number must be rounded down to the closest whole number.
The count of digits to which the numbers should be rounded (Mandatory Argument): That is the count to which the numbers should be rounded.
Utilization of ROUNDDOWN in a Sentence

Round up the value 1233.345 using the ROUNDDOWN function with one decimal place, two decimal places, the nearest number, the nearer 10, the nearer 100, and the nearer 1000, respectively.
To round off 1233.345, move the decimal point forward by one place. =ROUNDDOWN (A1, 1)

B1		✕	✓	f_x	=ROUNDDOWN(A1,1)	
	A	B		C	D	E
1	1233.345	1233.3				
2						

Round up 1233.345 to the nearest thousandth, and then insert it into =ROUNDUP (A1, -3)

B1		✕	✓	f_x	=ROUNDDOWN(A1,-3)	
	A	B		C	D	E
1	1233.345	1000				
2						

Sorting Function
The result of a column may be sorted using the Sort function in either an ascending or descending order, depending on user preference. The SORT function makes use of the statements that were presented before.

=SORT (array, [sort_index], [sort_order], [by col])

(Important counterargument) This set, or sequence contains the value that must be removed from consideration.
The sort of index is the name of the supplemental argument. It specifies which row or column needs to be sorted first.
(Supplementary Argument): Arrange the items in the desired order. This is the number used to sort the cells; a value of 1 implies ascending order, while a value of -1 suggests downward order. If you skip this section, it will automatically arrange in ascending order if you return to it later.
By col is the supplemental argument for this. This defines how the sorting will proceed; if it is FALSE, the rows will be filtered, and if it is TRUE, the columns will be sorted.
Application of SORT Function
Make sure the cells in the following table are arranged in ascending order using the SORT algorithm.

D2		▼	:	

	A	B
1	Item	Qty.
2	Apples	38
3	Cherries	29
4	Grapes	31
5	Lemons	34
6	Oranges	36
7	Peaches	25
8	Pears	40

Follow the steps below to sort things in ascending order, beginning with the least significant item, and working your way up to the most significant one.
You may try entering the function (=SORT), the source array (A2:B8), the sort index (2), and the sort order variable (1). By clicking on it, type =SORT (A2:B8, 2, 1) into an empty cell. This will be the formula that is applied.

D2		▼	:	=SORT(A2:B8, 2, 1)

	A	B
1	Item	Qty.
2	Apples	38
3	Cherries	29
4	Grapes	31
5	Lemons	34
6	Oranges	36
7	Peaches	25
8	Pears	40

After you hit the Enter key, the data will be evaluated in a rising fashion.

D2   =SORT(A2:B8, 2, 1)

	A	B	C	D	E
1	Item	Qty.		Item	Qty.
2	Apples	38		Peaches	25
3	Cherries	29		Cherries	29
4	Grapes	31		Grapes	31
5	Lemons	34		Lemons	34
6	Oranges	36		Oranges	36
7	Peaches	25		Apples	38
8	Pears	40		Pears	40

To arrange things in descending order, from the highest to the lowest possible value.
Simply clicking on the feature that needs to be utilized will place it into an empty cell. The sort order (A2:B8), the sort of index (2), and the sort order (1). To sum everything up, =SORT (A2:B8, 2, - 1).

D2   =SORT(A2:B8, 2, -1)

	A	B	C
1	Item	Qty.	
2	Apples	38	
3	Cherries	29	
4	Grapes	31	
5	Lemons	34	
6	Oranges	36	
7	Peaches	25	
8	Pears	40	

When you hit the Enter key, the data will be arranged in ascending manner.

D2   =SORT(A2:B8, 2, -1)

	A	B	C	D	E
1	Item	Qty.		Item	Qty.
2	Apples	38		Pears	40
3	Cherries	29		Apples	38
4	Grapes	31		Oranges	36
5	Lemons	34		Lemons	34
6	Oranges	36		Grapes	31
7	Peaches	25		Cherries	29
8	Pears	40		Peaches	25

The SORT function: Important Information You Need to Know
Using the first column as an example, the SORT technique sorts the values, so they are arranged in ascending order.
The SORT function is only available to users subscribed to Microsoft 365.
The result is dynamically recalculated whenever the underlying data undergo any modification.

14.2 Statistical Functions in Excel

A function known as the statistical function is one that, when applied to a group of cells inside a worksheet, executes various mathematical operations or processes. Statistical functions have been a part of Excel since its 2013 iteration and every version after then. Instances include COUNT, COUNTA, AVERAGE and various statistical functions.
COUNT Function
The COUNT function calculates the total inputs that include figures and the total number of cells that contain numbers.
The following are the parameters that are accepted by the COUNT function:
Value1 (Required Argument): The cell range for which you want to count those with figures. This is the range that you need to provide.
Value2... (Optional Argument): Currently, you can store 255 more objects, numerical values, or spans that count digits within.
Applying COUNT
Let's use the COUNT function to determine how many cells in the table contain numbers and then list them down.

Select a blank cell, enter the function's name, followed by the parameters. =COUNT (A2:B5)

Once you press your Enter key, the result will be the number 3.

Remember to keep all these points in your mind when working with the COUNT tool.

The COUNT functionality counts the number of arguments that include either numbers or text that symbolizes numbers, such as dates or numerals.

The COUNT function does not count textual errors or parameters that have values associated with them.

When counting logical values, the COUNTA function should be used.

If you want to count numbers based on certain factors, you should use the COUNTAIF or IF function.

The COUNT function pretends to count TRUE and FALSE as rational values even if it does not do so.

When a statement is an array or an index, the only tallied numbers are those found in the reference or database.

COUNTIF Function

Calculating the number of cells that meet certain requirements may be accomplished with the help of the COUNTIF function. Counting the number of cells containing text, dates, or numbers is another use for that technology. This feature also allows for logical operators and wildcard characters in expressions.

The following list is comprised of the parameters that are sent to the COUNTIF function:

= TAKE A COUNT (Range, criteria)

Range (Required Argument): This parameter identifies the cell range that will be included in the output.

Criteria (Compulsory Argument): This is the requirement that each cell in the worksheet must fulfill to be considered acceptable. The following are some examples of criteria in their many forms:

Examples of numerical values include integer, decimal, temporal, and logical values.

A text string comprising of one or even more wildcard characters (such as an asterisk or question mark), such as Monday, East, or Price.

Application of COUNTIF

Using the COUNTIF function, let's quickly determine how many times James' name appears in the below column.

	A	B	C	D
1	YEAR	NAMES		
2	2001	James		
3	2002	James		
4	2003	Peter		
5	2004	Jasmine		
6	2006	Gregg		

Follow the instructions below to determine how many times James' name appears on the page.
Find a space that isn't being utilized and write the name of the function there, followed by the parameters that will be applied.
=COUNTIF (B2:B6, "James") "James"

SEARCH		:	×	✓	f_x	=COUNTIF(B2:B6, "James")	

	A	B	C	D	E	F
1	YEAR	NAMES				
2	2001	James	=COUNTIF(B2:B6, "James")			
3	2002	James	COUNTIF(range, criteria)			
4	2003	Peter				
5	2004	Jasmine				
6	2006	Gregg				

Remember these points when you are working with the COUNTIF tool.
Make sure that the criteria statement is wrapped in quotation marks using the COUNTIF function; for instance, "James."
If the specified criteria statement is a text string, and that text string is larger than 255 characters, then the #VALUE ERROR error will occur.
A #VALUE error occurs in a group of cells in a workbook that has been closed if a formula refers to a cell or a range of cells in that workbook.

Average Function
The AVERAGE equation will be used to calculate the arithmetic mean of several parameters in a worksheet that will be provided.
The AVERAGE function accepts an unlimited number of parameters, which may be cell references, ranges, arrays, or constants. The maximum number of arguments is 255.
The AVERAGE function receives the inputs that have been presented so far:
Number1 (Required Argument): This is the first number in a cell relation or set that should be used to calculate the group average.
Number2 (Supplementary Argument): There are any additional numbers, cell comparisons, or ranges for which the average should be computed, with a maximum of 255 characters allowed in the calculation.

Application of Average
Find the arithmetic mean of the prices of the goods listed in the table below by using the equation labeled "AVERAGE."

D16		:	×	✓	f_x		

	A	B	C	D
1	COUNTRIES	GOODS SOLD		
2	GHANA	400		
3	NIGERIA	600		
4	KENYA	698		
5	GAMBIA	543		
6				

Please follow the procedures below and then use the AVERAGE function to get the average price of the goods sold.
Complete the missing cell with the function name and the parameters by typing them in.
=AVERAGE (B2:B5)
Remember these points when you are working with the AVERAGE function.
The function AVERAGE does not consider empty cells in its calculations.
The AVERAGE function will not consider cell reference statements with text or logical values in their arguments. On the other hand, the cells that have a value of zero will be counted.
For the cell relation arguments to make sense, you need to use numbers.
As a component of an estimate, counting logical values and text representations of numbers via the AVERAGE function.
To calculate the average value of any characteristic that satisfies a predetermined set of requirements or parameters, you need to use the AVERAGE IF or AVERAGE IFS function.

Chapter 15: Use of Five Advanced Excel Pivot Table Techniques
Once you've mastered the fundamentals of data summarization using pivot tables, you'll be ready to move on to more complex applications of the tool. What a terrific accomplishment!
Sure, you just scratched the surface of what you can accomplish with pivot tables when you only covered the basics. Now that you have a firm footing, you'll go through some additional features and tools you can utilize with your pivot tables to maximize their effectiveness.

In other words, do you have the elbow grease to get your hands filthy with some more advanced pivot table techniques? Okay, let's go right in.

15.1 Slicers

Although the word "slicer" may conjure up images of unusual forms of torture, it is, in fact, a valuable tool for analyzing large datasets; therefore, being acquainted with it is a must.

The term "slicer" doesn't seem to apply. Simply put, it's a method for connecting many pivot tables such that a single change to the filter affects all the linked tables.

Let's pretend that Jason is comparing two pivot tables: one showing quarterly beer sales and the other showing sales broken down by size. Currently, he is comparing his 2016 and 2017 information.

Sum of Gallons Sold	Column Labels				
Row Labels	Amber	IPA	Pilsner	Stout	Grand Total
Q1	1700	1100	600	2100	5500
Q2	1600	1100	1100	1800	5600
Q3	1900	1100	1600	1600	6200
Q4	2000	1300	800	2300	6400
Grand Total	7200	4600	4100	7800	23700

Sum of Gallons Sold	Column Labels				
Row Labels	Amber	IPA	Pilsner	Stout	Grand Total
6 pack	2520	920	615	2340	6395
Growler	1080	920	205	780	2985
Barrel	2160	920	1640	1560	6280
Half Barrel	1440	1840	1640	3120	8040
Grand Total	7200	4600	4100	7800	23700

He is interested in breaking out 2016 beer sales by size and quarter. Create a year slicer, so he doesn't have to keep going back and forth between the two pivot tables to adjust the year filter. How to do this is as follows:

1. Navigate to the innermost part of a pivot table.

Choose "Insert," and then pick the "Slicer" option. Click "OK" after choosing the variable (the year in this example) by which you would like to sort the data.

Third, modify the slicer's size and placement to where you want it to appear. Please put it on top of existing pivot tables so you can see the whole picture briefly.

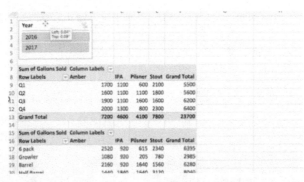

Fourth, Jason must connect his current pivot tables to the selected slicer to ensure that all data is properly linked. Select "Report Connections" from the slicer's context menu, then pick the pivot tables you want to be linked to it.

If Jason just wants to view data for 2016, he can easily filter out the other years' worth of data by clicking the 2016 button on the slicer. Setting up the slicer takes some time, but it will save you a lot of time and effort in the long run, especially if you deal with several pivot tables.

Year					
2016					
2017					

Sum of Gallons Sold	Column Labels				
Row Labels	Amber	IPA	Pilsner	Stout	Grand Total
Q1	800	500	250	1000	2550
Q2	750	500	500	850	2600
Q3	900	500	750	750	2900
Q4	1000	600	400	1000	3000
Grand Total	3450	2100	1900	3600	11050

Sum of Gallons Sold	Column Labels				
Row Labels	Amber	IPA	Pilsner	Stout	Grand Total
6 pack	1207.5	420	285	1080	2992.5
Growler	517.5	420	95	360	1392.5
Barrel	1035	420	760	720	2935
Half Barrel	690	840	760	1440	3730

15.2 Timelines

Filtering by date may be done rapidly using timelines, which are interactive filters. They streamline the process of seeing PivotTable data for a custom time range. They function similarly to slicers, which may be inserted once and updated alongside the Pivot Table.

Inserting a Timeline
To access a specific cell in the Pivot Table, select it and click OK.
Select the ribbon's Analyze tab.
The Insert Timeline option should be selected.
With PivotCharts and cube analyses, you can now include a Timeline.
A dialogue window titled "Insert Timelines" pops up. The PivotTable's date fields are identified automatically and displayed for your convenience. There is usually just one field to choose from.
Just click on the appropriate drop-down menu to create a timeline based on a certain date range.
Just go ahead and hit the OK button.

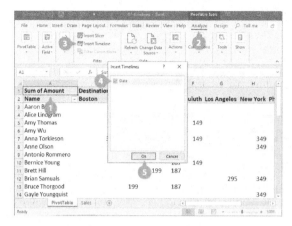

The PivotTable will only show data from the selected period in the Timeline.

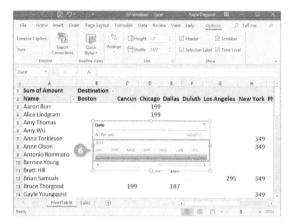

A multi-selection may be made by either clicking and dragging along the timeline or by clicking the first interval to be included, holding the Shift key, and then clicking the final period to be included.

15.3 Tabular View

Compact Form, the default structure for Pivot Tables, shows all row elements in a single column and allocates greater space to numerical data. In contrast, tabular forms show one column for each field & provide room for field labels.
The techniques below will elaborate you how to export your Pivot Table design to Tabular format:
To begin, choose a cell in the Pivot Table.

Region	Ave of Salary
⊟ F	$77,994
North	$80,268
East	$82,027
South	$83,677
West	$67,348
⊟ M	$81,908
North	$62,631
East	$78,063
South	$86,904
West	$87,438
Grand Total	$79,840

Two, choose the "Design" tab on the Ribbon.

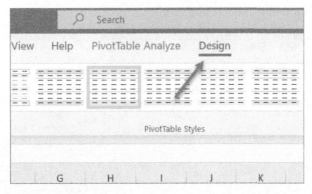

Third, go to the Layout tab and choose "Report Layout."

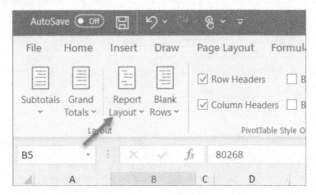

To see the data in a table, choose that option in the fourth step's drop-down menu.

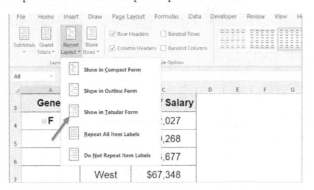

A tabular form will replace the Pivot table in Step 5.

Gener	Region	Ave of Salary
⊟F	North	$80,268
	East	$82,027
	South	$83,677
	West	$67,348
F Total		$77,994
⊟M	North	$62,631
	East	$78,063
	South	$86,904
	West	$87,438
M Total		$81,908
Grand Total		$79,840

15.4 Calculated Fields

By now, you should know that Excel is a formidable calculating tool, and the ability to generate a conceptual data model is a skill you'll need when dealing with pivot tables.

You may use a calculated field in a pivot table the same way you would a plug-in formula in a regular spreadsheet to ensure that a calculation is applied consistently throughout the whole table.

Jason needs to calculate his earnings for his four beer varieties (Pilsner, Stout, Amber, and IPA). Without a pivot table, he would have to manually remove Q1 costs from Q1 sales, Q2 costs from Q2 sales, and so on, which would be time-consuming and error-prone. He may use a calculated field to automatically determine his earnings from selling each kind of beer. The procedure is as follows: When you have a cell selected in the pivot table, go to the "Pivot Table Analyze" tab on the ribbon, click the "Fields, Items, & Sets" button, then select "Calculated Field."

2. In the resulting window, give the new computed field a name (Jason may call it "profit" or something like that).

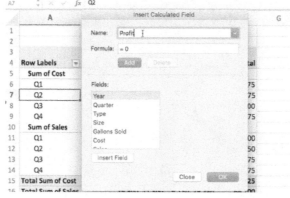

Third, Jason must now input the calculation formula. He is aware of the formula for calculating profit, which is as follows: cost minus revenue. To do this, he would first choose "sales," then "Insert Field," put a negative sign, select "Cost," and repeat the process.

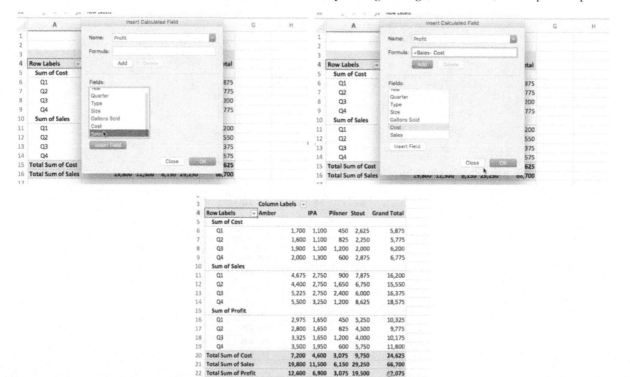

		Column Labels				
Row Labels		Amber	IPA	Pilsner	Stout	Grand Total
Sum of Cost						
Q1		1,700	1,100	450	2,625	5,875
Q2		1,600	1,100	825	2,250	5,775
Q3		1,900	1,100	1,200	2,000	6,200
Q4		2,000	1,300	600	2,875	6,775
Sum of Sales						
Q1		4,675	2,750	900	7,875	16,200
Q2		4,400	2,750	1,650	6,750	15,550
Q3		5,225	2,750	2,400	6,000	16,375
Q4		5,500	3,250	1,200	8,625	18,575
Sum of Profit						
Q1		2,975	1,650	450	5,250	10,325
Q2		2,800	1,650	825	4,500	9,775
Q3		3,325	1,650	1,200	4,000	10,175
Q4		3,500	1,950	600	5,750	11,800
Total Sum of Cost		7,200	4,600	3,075	9,750	24,625
Total Sum of Sales		19,800	11,500	6,150	29,250	66,700
Total Sum of Profit		12,600	6,900	3,075	19,500	42,075

The bottom row of Jason's pivot table now displays the calculated field calculating his revenue for every beer and the total profit.

15.5 Recommended Pivot Tables

Suppose you find it too cumbersome to create a new pivot table using the Quick Analytical model in Excel 2022. In that case, you may quickly produce a pivot table using the new Suggested Pivot Tables command button. Here are the simple procedures to implement this method:

- You may start making a new pivot table by clicking on a cell within the data list.
- Any cell inside the table will do, so long as your data collection has a string of column headings followed by a row of data.
- To use this feature, either use the Alt+NSP keyboard shortcut or click the Recommended PivotTables button on Insert tab of your Ribbon.
- A suggestion box in Excel will appear if you click the Recommended PivotTables button. Just on the left side of this dialogue box, you'll see examples of the several types of pivot tables Excel 2013 can generate based on the data within your list.
- Inside the list view on the left, choose the kind of pivot table you wish to create, and then hit OK.

When you select OK, Excel copies the chosen pivot table into its worksheet (Sheet1) and moves it to the head of your workbook. When you pick this pivot table on the new sheet, the Pivot Table Parameters task pane and PivotTable Techniques contextual tab appear on the right side of an Excel worksheet window.

The new pivot table may be modified using the controls in the task pane & the contextual tab.

Chapter 16: Create Charts in Excel: Types and Examples

Excel charts allow you to visually examine the data on your worksheet by showing it as rows and columns of bars on a chart. This makes it possible for you to make more informed decisions. There is a wide variety of graphical representations available to choose from when presenting the findings of an investigation. A pie chart, a line chart, a bar chart, and a column chart are just a few examples of the charts available in Excel.

Graphed data is more interesting to look at, may be heard, and is simpler to read and understand. You will investigate the data and use charts to look for inconsistencies between the different numbers.

16.1 Types of Charts

Excel has various charts; however, you will review a few in this chapter.

Column Charts

In this graph, the horizontal axis's divisions contrast with the vertical axes. There are several subtypes of column charts: stacked columns, clustered columns, stacked columns in three dimensions, and others.

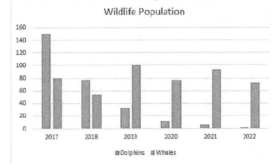

Line Chart

This graph illustrates the progression of data across a range of periods, including months, years, days, and so on. Other line maps are available, such as stacks of line maps with arrows and stacks covering 100 percent of the screen.

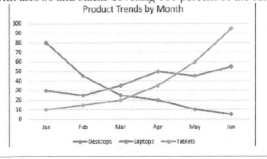

Bar Chart

Much like a column chart, a bar chart links the groupings on the horizontal axis to the data on the vertical axis. There are a extensive variety of distinct styles. The bar map is used for large-label messaging. Clustered bar charts, stacked bar charts, and three-dimensional bar charts are examples of the many forms of bar charts.

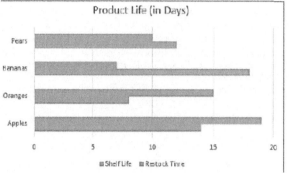

Pie Chart

It is a graph that illustrates or describes findings using a circular graph. This graph displays the data and specifications via a pie slice layout.

Doughnut Chart

It is a graph that displays how parts relate to the whole, and much like a pie chart, when all the pieces are put together, the result is 100%. This graph was created to show how the parts link to the total. The doughnut pie chart, in contrast to the pie chart, can only store one data series simultaneously and many data series simultaneously.

16.2 How to Insert Charts in Excel?

Select any data to be incorporated in the graphic.

Select Insert after making your selection from the drop-down menu containing Recommended Charts.

Pick a chart to look at from the list of charts that have been recommended.

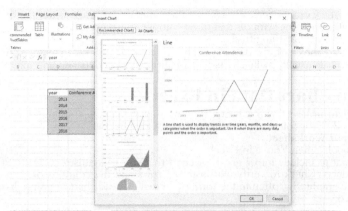

After you have made your selection, you may go on to the next step by clicking the OK button.

Giving a title to Chart

After giving the Chart a name, anybody who takes a cursory glance at the Excel spreadsheet you have created will be able to identify or recall the purpose of the Chart. To give your Chart a title, do the steps listed below:
It is possible to click on any part of the chart area.

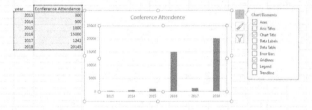

Click the addition symbol that is in the top right-hand corner of the Table.
The following step is to pick the Chart title from the list of available alternatives.

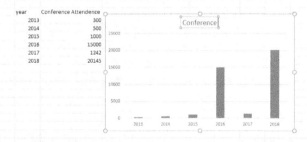

Simply pressing anywhere within the textbox will allow you to choose a different title in place of the current Chart Title.

16.3 Top Five Excel Graph and Chart Best Practices

If you use different methods, you'll be able to make the most of the built-in style and formatting possibilities that Excel provides for your charts. To maximize the usefulness of your diagrams, it is suggested that you follow these guidelines:

- Get Your House in Order: Graphs that are densely colored or include a lot of text might be distracting and difficult to comprehend. Get rid of irrelevant or unnecessary information, so your audience can focus on what it is you're attempting to convey to them.
- Choosing the Appropriate Subjects: It is important to choose a theme suitable for your target demographic, the nature of the information being presented, and the overarching purpose of the chart. Experiment with several methods but commit to the one most suited to completing the work.
- Make Effective Use of the Text: There is a fair probability that you will include some text in addition to the graphs and charts you create (such as axis or title labels). You must write concisely while yet using descriptive language, and you should also pay attention to how any information you write is produced.

- Take Care to Organize the Components: Always pay close attention to the positioning of the visuals, such as the names of the components in a diagram or the symbols that those components represent. They shouldn't take away from the readability of your graph but contribute something fresh.
- Before beginning to create the chart, the data should be sorted in the following manner: After organizing the data or getting rid of duplicates, individuals usually make charts that are difficult to understand and might result in errors.

16.4 How You can Chart Data in Excel

To begin creating a graph or chart in Excel, you will first need to import the data you intend to display into the program. Create a chart using the data using Excel 2022 by following the directions provided below.

Step 1: Enter the Data into your Worksheet

Choose to Open a New Workbook When You're in Excel.

Create a list of the data you want to include into a graph or chart that you will construct. From 2013 to 2017, you will analyze the revenue generated by five products. Check to verify that both the rows and the columns of your table have labels. After that, the information may be represented graphically, often in the form of an easy-to-read chart or graph. You are free to experiment with the sample data that I have provided.

Product	2013	2014	2015	2016	2017
Product A	$18,580	$49,225	$16,326	$10,017	$26,134
Product B	$78,970	$82,262	$48,640	$48,640	$48,640
Product C	$24,236	$131,390	$79,022	$71,009	$81,474
Product D	$16,730	$19,730	$12,109	$11,355	$17,686
Product E	$35,358	$42,685	$20,893	$16,065	$21,388

Step 2: Select Range for Creating Graph or Chart from your Workbook Data

You may choose the data you want to include in your graph by clicking and dragging the mouse over the cells. This will bring up a menu.

After you have chosen a chart type, the cells in your selected range will be highlighted in a grey color.

Excel 2022 will teach you how to make a cluster column chart if you want to learn how to do it. In the following part, you will be led through making a clustered columns chart in Excel, starting with the basics, and running your way up to more advanced topics.

How can you Make a Chart with your Excel?

You will be able to choose the kind of chart you want to use after you have completed the steps of entering your data and selecting the cell range you want to work with. In this part, you will develop clustered column charts by using the data from the example that came before this one as a starting point.

Step 1: Select a Chart Type

Select the Include tab from the top banner of the window after highlighting the data you want to insert once you have done so in the Workbook. About in the middle of the toolbar is an area dedicated to charting with several different options. Excel provides Suggested Charts based on popularity, but you can select a different layout by choosing any dropdown boxes. In addition to that, Excel offers Recommended Charts.

Step 2: Create the Chart

Click the column chart icon that can be found under the Insert tab, and then choose the Clustered Column option from the drop-down menu that appears.

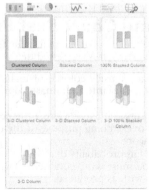

Excel will create a cluster chart column for you, which will do automatically depending on the data you provide in the spreadsheet. The chart will be in the part that is in the center of your worksheet.

Double-click the text that reads "Chart Title" on the chart, and then type a name into the box that appears. This will give your chart a name. This graph will be referred to as the "Product Profit 2013-2017" chart.

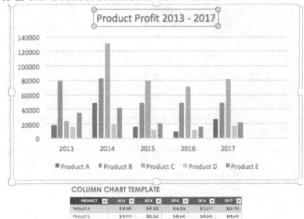

COLUMN CHART TEMPLATE

PRODUCT OVERVIEW

The two tabs on the toolbar, Chart Design and Chart Format, are the ones you will use to modify your chart. By selecting the option labeled "Chart Design," you can access both tabs. Excel will automatically apply design, style, and format options to graphs and charts; however, you can add additional customization by looking at the tabs. Excel will apply these choices to graphs and charts. After that, you will methodically go through all the Chart Design adjustments available to you step by step.

Home	Insert	Page Layout	Formulas	Data	Review	View	Chart Design	Format

Step 3: Adding your Chart Elements
Adding chart components to your graph or chart will seem to be of higher quality since these components will make the data more understandable or give more information. You can choose a chart element by heading to the top left corner of the screen and clicking on the dropdown menu labeled Add Chart Element (underneath your home tab).

- Axes
- Axis Titles
- Chart Title
- Data Labels
- Data Table
- Error Bars
- Gridlines
- Legend
- Lines
- Trendline
- Up/Down Bars

To Hide or Display Axes:
Select Axes. If you provide a cell range, Excel will automatically fill your chart with horizontal and vertical axes based on the column and row headers of the cells in that range.

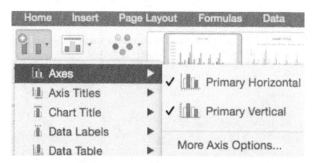

Unchecking these boxes will remove the axis that is shown on the chart. In this illustration, selecting Primary Horizontal would result in removing the year labels from the x plane of the chart.

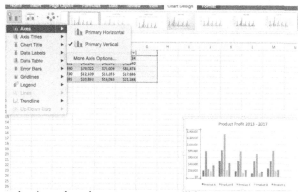

By selecting More Axis Options from the Axes dropdown menu, you will have access to more text and formatting options, such as the ability to insert tick marks, numbers, and labels or change the size ans color of your text.

To Add the Axis Titles:
After selecting the Add Chart Element button, go to the dropdown menu next to that button and choose Axis Title. Because Excel does not instantly add axis names to your chart, the checkboxes for Primary Horizontal and Primary Vertical will be unchecked by default.

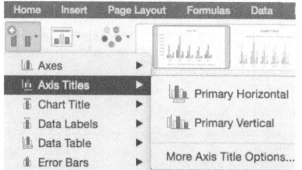

Simply clicking on the text box on your chart enables you to generate names for the Primary Vertical or Primary Horizontal axes, respectively. In this example, you utilized both of your mouse buttons. Enter the axes' names into the appropriate fields. This illustration now includes the terms "Year" (along the horizontal axis) and "Profit" (along the vertical axis).

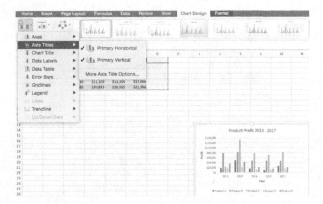

To Move or Remove Chart Title:

Add a Chart Element and choose Chart Title from the drop-down menu. You can select none, place the overlay above the chart, put it in the middle of the screen, or select extra title options.

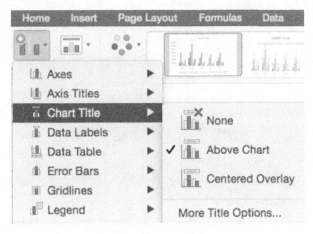

Select None from the drop-down menu to remove the chart title.

When you pick the option to Display Above Chart, the title will show above the chart. Excel will automatically set the chart title in the appropriate location if a chart is generated.

By selecting Centered Overlay from the Format option, you can ensure that the title is centered inside the chart's gridlines. Be wary of this option since you do not want the title to conceal any information in the graph and make it challenging to read (as shown in the example below).

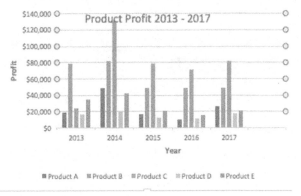

To Add the Data Labels:

Click the right mouse button, then choose "Data Labels." There are six different ways to label data: none (the default option), the center, the inside end, the outside end, the inner base, and additional variations.

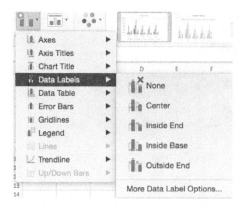

You can select one of these four ways to label each data point that is measured. Click on the option that you want to choose it. This adjustment might be handy if you have a limited amount of correct data or a significant amount of spare space in your chart. When data labels are added to a cluster column chart, on the other hand, the chart is likely to seem as if it has too much going on. The following is an illustration of what it will look like when you choose Center data labels:

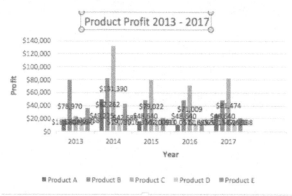

To Add the Data Table:

Click the Add Chart Element button and choose Data Table from the drop-down menu. There are 3 pre-formatted selections, as well as an additional menu that may be reached by selecting Additional Data Table Alternatives:

The data table is not duplicated here since it is not included in the graphic by default.
The data range is shown in the data table located below the visual and accessible via the Legend Keys. In addition, there will be a legend that uses a color-coding scheme.

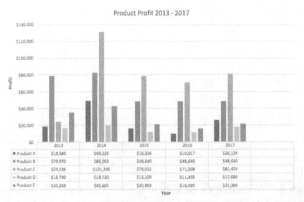

When the No Legend Keys are used, the data table behind the chart is still shown, but there is no legend to accompany it.

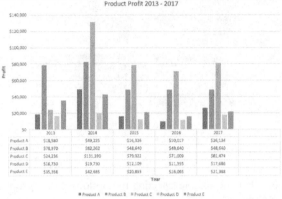

Because of this, you should most certainly expand the size of your chart if you want to include the data table in your presentation. Simply clicking and dragging one of the chart's corners will allow you to make it larger.

To Add the Error Bars:

After that, choose the Error Bars option from the Add Chart Element menu. In addition to these, you also have the choice of the following four alternatives: None (which is the default), Standard Error, 5 percent (Percentage), and Standard Deviation. Error bars may be added to the data to indicate the potential for inaccuracy. These error bars are calculated using traditional formulas for error and added to the data.

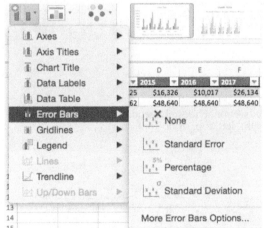

There is a broad variety of options available, and when you choose Standard Error, you will be represented with a chart comparable to the one shown above.

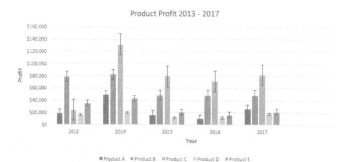

To Add the Gridlines:

After selecting "Add the Chart Element," you will then be able to see the Gridlines. As additional choices, there are also main major horizontals, primary major verticals, and primary minor verticals. When you create a column chart in Excel, the program will automatically include a Primary Major Horizontal gridline.

You can choose any number of gridlines that you like by selecting the options. For example, the following is how your chart looks when all four of the available gridline options are applied.

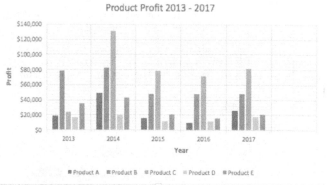

To Add the Legend:

After that, under the Add Chart Element section, choose Legend from the drop-down option. You can place the legends in any one of these five different positions: none, right, left, top, or bottom.

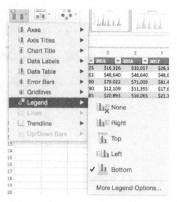

The location of the legend should be determined by the kind of chart and its format. Make use of the chart to help you choose the alternative that gives the impression of being the most pleasing to the eye. You are presented with the chart above when you choose the Right legend position.

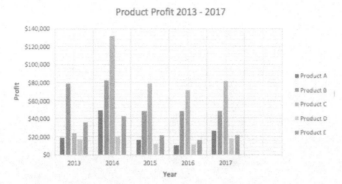

Cluster Column Charts do not have access to Lines in their chart type. You may add lines to the chart by selecting the appropriate option in other chart types where you only compare two variables. These lines include goals, references, averages, and other similar information.

To Add the Trendline:
You may add a trendline to a chart by choosing Trendline after clicking the Add Chart Element button. In addition to Some additional Trendline Alternatives, you can choose None, which is the
default option. You may also select Linear Forecast, Linear, Exponential, or Moving Average. Check to verify that you have chosen the appropriate one for your data batch. In this instance, you will utilize Linear.

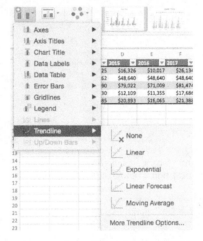

Excel will automatically create the trendline for you to use when comparing five different things across time. To create a linear trendline of Product A, choose Product A, then select the blue OK symbol from the toolbar.

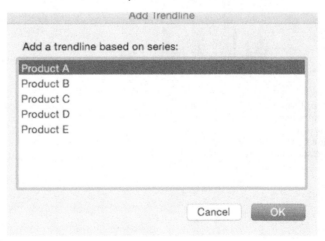

The graph shows the linear progression of Product A as a dotted trendline as you advance. In addition, a legend item for Linear has been introduced in Excel (Product A).

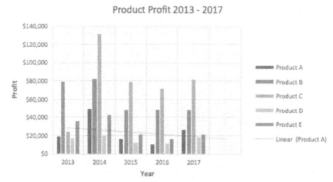

You can see the equation on your chart by double-clicking on the trendline. Select Open from the context menu that appears when you right-click the Format Trendline window. You must first tick a box at the bottom of the window to allow the display of equations on charts. The answer to the issue may be seen in your graph.

Please remember that you are free to include any number of distinct trendlines in the chart you are working on. The trendlines for Products A and C have been drawn out on the graph are being demonstrated here.

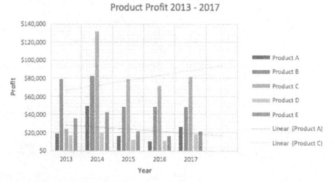

You will not have access to the Up/Down Bars feature while working with a column chart; however, you may utilize them inside a line chart to illustrate how data points have changed.

Step 4: Adjusting the Quick Layout

Using the Quick Layout option, located in the second dropdown menu of the toolbar, you may quickly and easily modify the order in which the objects in your chart are shown (legend, titles, clusters etc.).

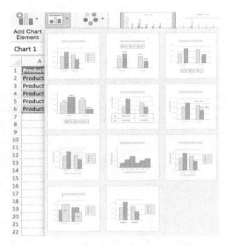

There are eleven different options for the quick layout. Simply moving your cursor over the options will give you additional information about them. After that, choose the option that you want to put into use.

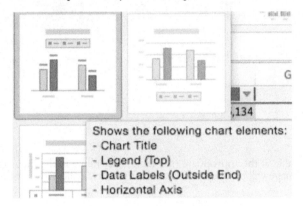

Step 5: Change the Colors
The next menu item on the toolbar is labeled "Change Colors." Simply clicking on the icon and selecting the color scheme will allow you to match the colors and design of your business.

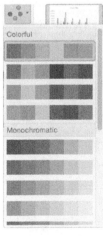

Step 6: Change the Style
There are 14 different kinds of cluster column charts available for your selection. Excel will use Style 1 by default, but you can choose one of the other styles if you want the chart to have a different appearance. If you click the right arrow in the photo bar, you'll see several options from which you may choose.

Step 7: Switch the Row/Column
You may switch the axis by clicking on the toolbar that says Switch Row/Column. When there are more than two variables shown in a chart, it is possible that switching the axes will not be immediately apparent.

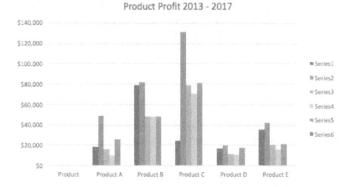

It's possible that you can modify the product and the year if you rearrange the columns and rows (profit remains over the y-axis). There are now legends with color coding to indicate which goods are categorized according to year (not product). To ensure there are no misunderstandings, click on the legend and change the series titles to the years.

Step 8: Selecting the Data
Click the Select Data button on the toolbar to update the data range.

There will be a door or window available at the appropriate moment. After filling in the range of cells you want to deal with, you will want to click the "Ok" button. The image will be updated to reflect this newly collected set of data.

Step 9: Changing the Chart Type
Choose a different kind of chart from the selection that drops below.

Excel gives you the option to choose from nine distinct kinds of charts to use. The chart type you choose must be compatible with the data you provide.

Gil B. Dreher

You can save the chart as a template by selecting the Save as Template option when you are prompted to do so.
You'll be able to give your template a name in the new window that just appeared. Excel will establish a folder dedicated only to storing your template files to simplify the process. Go ahead & click on button to save your work when you're ready.

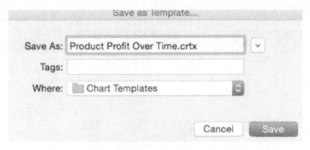

Step 10: Moving the Chart
Right-click the Move Chart icon on the toolbar, and then choose it from the available option.

Move
Chart

Charts may be arranged in several different ways within the new conversation box that has opened. Either make a new sheet and add this chart to it (New sheet) or place this chart in another sheet and utilize it as an item there (Place this chart in another sheet) (Object in). Click the right mouse button, then choose "OK."

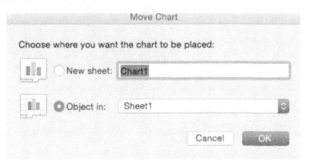

Step 11: Change the Formatting
The Format tab makes it simple to format the chart's components and the text inside it. With this tab, you can update the chart's color, shape, fill, size, and alignment and insert new shapes. Make a chart unique to your organization using the keyboard keys included in the Format tab (images, colors, etc.).

To change a particular chart element, go to the top left of your toolbar and click on the drop-down menu. Then, choose the element you want to modify.

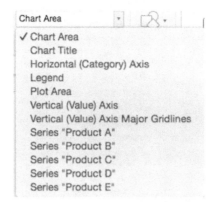

Step 12: Deleting the Chart

To delete a chart, select it and then click the Delete key on your keyboard. This is the quickest and easiest method.

How can you make the Graph into Excel

Because they all conduct comparable tasks, Excel classifies graphs under the umbrella term of "charts." The activities that are necessary to be taken to create a graph in Excel are listed below.

Select Range for Creating Graph from the Workbook Data

You may choose the data you want to include in the graph by clicking and dragging the mouse over the cells. This will bring up a menu.

Finding out how far your mobile phone can really reach has become a lot less complicated in recent years.

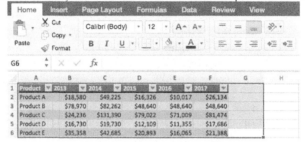

After the text has been selected, there is a large selection of graphs from which to pick (which Excel refer to as the chart). Choose the Recommended Charts toolbar from the Insert tab's list of available options. Then, click on the kind of graph you like to see to choose it.

You are now in possession of a chart. To customize your graph, you may utilize the processes described in the previous section. The capability for making a chart does not change while building a graph; it remains the same.

Chapter 17: Excel Table

Understanding is facilitated by visual representations of knowledge, notwithstanding the nature of the subject matter. This is helpful for numbers that need to be compared to one another. In this case, graphs are the most effective form of representation. Excel is going to be your primary working tool.

You will also acquire the knowledge and abilities necessary to create dynamic graphs and charts that automatically update themselves whenever the data they are based on is altered.

17.1 How to Create a Table in Excel?

For inserting a table, go out the actions that are listed below.

1. Select a cell randomly from data collection by clicking on it.

2) Select Table from the Tables submenu of the Insert tab.

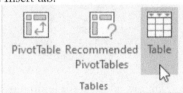

A box labeled Create Table pops up.
When you open Excel, it will automatically choose the information you need. Ensure the box next to "My table contains headers" is checked, and then hit OK.

Result. Excel will create a professional-looking table for you. You may still see this as a typical data range, but numerous advanced options are now only a button click away.

	Last Name	Sales	Country	Quarter	
2	Smith	$16,753.00	UK	Qtr 3	
3	Johnson	$14,808.00	USA	Qtr 4	
4	Williams	$10,644.00	UK	Qtr 2	
5	Jones	$1,390.00	USA	Qtr 3	
6	Brown	$4,865.00	USA	Qtr 4	
7	Williams	$12,438.00	UK	Qtr 1	
8	Johnson	$9,339.00	UK	Qtr 2	
9	Smith	$18,919.00	USA	Qtr 3	
10	Jones	$9,213.00	USA	Qtr 4	
11	Jones	$7,433.00	UK	Qtr 1	
12	Brown	$3,255.00	USA	Qtr 2	
13	Williams	$14,867.00	USA	Qtr 3	
14	Williams	$19,302.00	UK	Qtr 4	
15	Smith	$9,698.00	USA	Qtr 1	
16					

Sorting a Table
Follow these instructions to arrange the list such that Last Name appears first, and Sales comes second.
One may sort the sales data from smallest to largest by clicking the arrow adjacent to the sales column.
Then, choose Last Name from the drop-down menu and click the arrow to the right of the Sort A to Z button.
Result.

	A	B	C	D	E
1	Last Name	Sales	Country	Quarter	
2	Brown	$3,255.00	USA	Qtr 2	
3	Brown	$4,865.00	USA	Qtr 4	
4	Johnson	$9,339.00	UK	Qtr 2	
5	Johnson	$14,808.00	USA	Qtr 4	
6	Jones	$1,390.00	USA	Qtr 3	
7	Jones	$7,433.00	UK	Qtr 1	
8	Jones	$9,213.00	USA	Qtr 4	
9	Smith	$9,698.00	USA	Qtr 1	
10	Smith	$16,753.00	UK	Qtr 3	
11	Smith	$18,919.00	USA	Qtr 3	
12	Williams	$10,644.00	UK	Qtr 2	
13	Williams	$12,438.00	UK	Qtr 1	
14	Williams	$14,867.00	USA	Qtr 3	
15	Williams	$19,302.00	UK	Qtr 4	
16					

Filtering a Table

Here are the actions you need to take to filter a table.

1. Select "United States" from the drop-down menu next to "Country."

Result.

	A	B	C	D	E
1	Last Name	Sales	Country	Quarter	
2	Brown	$3,255.00	USA	Qtr 2	
3	Brown	$4,865.00	USA	Qtr 4	
5	Johnson	$14,808.00	USA	Qtr 4	
6	Jones	$1,390.00	USA	Qtr 3	
8	Jones	$9,213.00	USA	Qtr 4	
9	Smith	$9,698.00	USA	Qtr 1	
11	Smith	$18,919.00	USA	Qtr 3	
14	Williams	$14,867.00	USA	Qtr 3	
16					

Total Row

The following is what you'll do in order to have a sum row added at the bottom of your table.

1. Choose a table cell to work with. Select Total Row inside your Table Style Option subgroup on the Table Design tab.

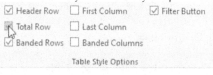

Result.

	A	B	C	D	E
1	Last Name	Sales	Country	Quarter	
2	Brown	$3,255.00	USA	Qtr 2	
3	Brown	$4,865.00	USA	Qtr 4	
5	Johnson	$14,808.00	USA	Qtr 4	
6	Jones	$1,390.00	USA	Qtr 3	
8	Jones	$9,213.00	USA	Qtr 4	
9	Smith	$9,698.00	USA	Qtr 1	
11	Smith	$18,919.00	USA	Qtr 3	
14	Williams	$14,867.00	USA	Qtr 3	
16	Total			8	
17					

Click each cell inside the final row to get the sum, count, average, etc. of a column. Try adding up the numbers in the Sales column as an illustration.

17.2 How to Make a Table with a Selected Style?

Select a random cell in the spreadsheet.

2. Select the Styles group and Format as Table on the Home tab.

Third, decide on a table format.

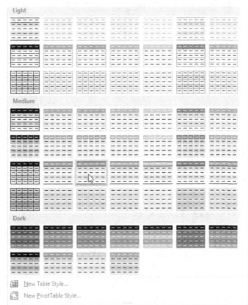

Note that you may make your table style by clicking New Table Style, or you can copy an existing table style by right-clicking it and selecting Duplicate. If you change the settings for a custom table style, it will affect all the tables in your workbook. A considerable time may be saved because of this.

Fourth, Excel can do the data selection for you automatically. Ensure the box next to "My table contains headers" is checked, and then hit OK.

Gil B. Dreher

Result. Another option for including a table.

Apply the following procedures to restore this table to a standard set of cells (while preserving the formatting).
Step 5: Pick a table cell to work with. Then, choose to Convert to Range from the Tools sub-group on the Table Design menu.

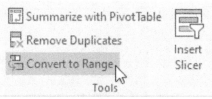

As a result, a tidy array of cells.

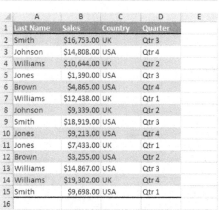

17.3 How to Name a Table in Excel?

When you create a table in Excel, it automatically gets a name that follows this pattern: Table1, Table 2, Table 3, etc. If you have many tables in a single worksheet, you may want to give each table a name.

Please note that all screenshots in this post were created using Excel 2016. If you're using a different version of Excel, the interface may seem different, but the features should be the same (until otherwise noted).

For renaming a table:

Pick the desk to click on.

Table Name may be found under Table Tools ➔ Design ➔ Properties.

Select Table ➔ Table Name on a Mac.

Select the table's name and replace it with a new one.

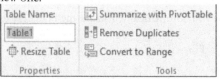

Tips:

In your Address bar, located to the left of your Formula bar, you'll see a list of all the tables you've created. The selected table will be brought up immediately, no matter where it is in the workbook.

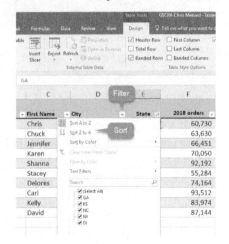

Important for names

Use valid characters — First characters of names must be either letters or the underscore (_) or backslash () characters. The remainder of the name should consist of periods, letters, numbers, and underscores.

Exceptions: If you try to use the letters "C," "c," "R," or "r" for such a name, Excel will instead utilize those letters as a shortcut to go to the row or column corresponding to the currently selected cell.

Don't utilize cell references — No names, including Z$100 or R1C1, are allowed to be identical to cell references.

To avoid misunderstanding, please don't use a gap between words — Any name, including a space, will be rejected. The use of spaces in the name should be something to think about. You may also separate words with the underscore (_) or period (.). Division of Sales, Tax on Sales, and First Quarter are all examples.

Maximum of 255 characters — The maximum length for a table name is 255 characters.

Use unique table names — There must not be any name repetitions. If you type "Sales," but there's already a name named "SALES" in the same document, you'll be requested to choose a new name since Excel doesn't differentiate between upper- & lower-case characters in names.

17.4 How to Use Tables in Excel?

Filters

When you develop a table, the 1st thing you will see is that its headers have filtering controls built right in. Click the arrow in the column header of the table that you wish to filter by, and a drop-down menu will appear. In the Table Tools design tab, select the box labeled Show Filter Button if you don't want to show the filter options.

Sorting

You may rapidly sort information by any column using the filter arrows. Data Sort allows you to sort by many fields simultaneously.

Easy Data Entries for PivotTables and Charts

When data is added to a chart's data range after the chart has been produced, the chart will not update to reflect the new data. However, when data is added to a table, the table will expand to incorporate the new data, and the chart will update accordingly.

It's also useful for populating new columns with information. The first 2 months of the year are in B1 and C1; thus, moving March to D1 will refresh the graph.

Can you utilize PivotTables? You can easily refresh your Pivot Table after adding new data to your table. If you're using a data range, modify Data Source to include the additional information.

Automatic AutoFill

Whenever you put a new entry to a table, not only will the formatting expand, but the table will also immediately AutoFill any formulae in the table. This happens whenever you add a new record. This helps save a significant amount of time.

Calculated Columns

It's one of my all-time favorite songs. Is there a need to fill in a formula inside a bare cell? Excel's calculated columns will fill in the remaining rows of an empty table column when a formula is entered. Compared to AutoFill, this is quick.

Use computed columns to further minimize mistakes in a dataset of 500 thousand rows or more. Calculated columns, as described in Step 4, update, and append your formula whenever you add or remove data from the table, so your work is never done.

The good news continues: if you want to alter the formula inside a computed column, you need to do it in a single cell (it might be the very last cell in a column), and the update will propagate to all rows.

Headers always available

When using a dataset, the row containing the range's heading disappears as you go down the spreadsheet. The table's header row is always displayed when a table is created, regardless of whether the Freeze Panes option is selected from the View menu.

Total Row

Place your cursor anywhere in the table, then choose Total Row from the Table Tool menu. Each cell within the sum row has a drop-down arrow that allows you to use built-in functions.

Quick Formatting

The Table Styles subtab of the Table Utilities design menu is where you'll find all the options you need. One of the quickest methods of data formatting is this. After settling on a theme, you may further customize your table's appearance using Banded Rows & Banded Columns. First Column & Last Column will give you more possibilities for formatting.

Automatic Naming

Names are generated mechanically when using a table for computations.

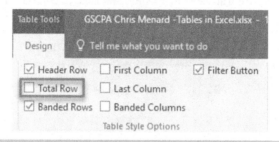

State	2018 Sales	2019 Sales	Variance
GA	66,451	67,781	=[@[2019 Sales]]-[@[2018 Sales]]
KS	70,050	72,152	
GA	60,730	62,552	
TX	83,974	83,135	
NC	74,164	73,423	

Quick Totals

When creating a table, selecting Total Row from Table Tools Design will allow you to include a row with the sum of the table's data. It's never been simpler to do several Excel tasks than with the help of the Total Row.

17.5 How to Sort a Table in Excel?

Sorting is a frequent method used in the field of data management. To sort a table in Excel, you may choose one or more columns, an ascending or descending sort, or create a custom sort.

Sorting your table

Pick a data cell to focus on.

To use this feature, go to the Menu Bar and choose Home ➔ Sort & Filter.

You may also go to Data ➔ Sort.

Make a choice:

Select a column and click "Sort A to Z" to arrange its contents alphabetically.

Selecting "Sort Z to A" will reverse the column's sort order.

Using the Custom Sort function, sorting in several columns using user-defined criteria is possible.

Methods for implementing a user-defined sort are as follows:

Make use of the Personalized Ordering option.

Choose the "Add Level" option.

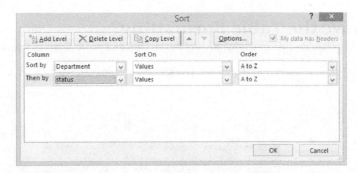

Choose a column you need to sort using the drop-down menu labeled Column, and then choose the column you need to sort from the menu labeled Then by. For instance, you may sort "Status" after "Department."
Select Values for Sort On.
For Order, choose from alphabetical, largest to smallest, and reverse order.
You may repeat steps 2–5 for any additional column you wish to sort.
Delete Level is the option you'll want to use if you want to get rid of a level.
If your data contains a header row, choose the My data includes headers checkbox.
Click the OK button.

17.6 How to Extend a Table in Excel?

Once you've established a table in Excel, you may modify its layout by adding or removing rows and columns.
To expand a table in Excel, utilize the Resize function.
After selecting a cell in a table, the Table Tools menu will display.
Modify the table size by selecting the option in the Design menu.

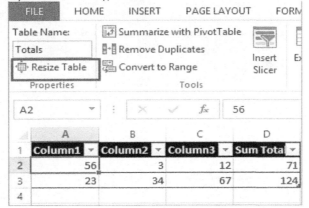

Starting at the upper-left cell, choose the complete set of cells you wish to include in your table.
To illustrate, the following is an original table that includes cells A1:C5. After expanding it by another two columns & three rows, your table can now accommodate data in cells A1 through E8.

To temporarily conceal the Resize Table dialogue box while you pick the range just on a worksheet, click Collapse Dialog first.
When you've decided on a suitable range for your table, click the OK button.

17.7 How to Remove the Table Formatting?

This is how you can strip a table in Excel of its styling while keeping its data and other features intact:
Pick a table cell at random.
Select None, the first style in the Light group upon that Table Design tab's Table Styles group.

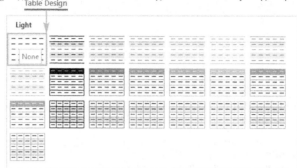

You may also choose Clear underneath your table styles or use the More button ⬇ in the Table Styles group.

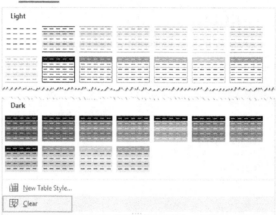

You'll have a perfectly working Excel table, albeit one devoid of formatting.

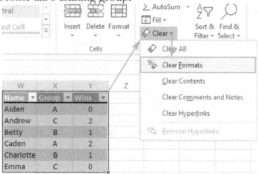

Tips and notes: Both choices eliminate the default formatting with the table style, not the formatting you've applied yourself.
This approach is helpful when you need the table's features but want to preserve the current formatting in the cells. Your data may be easily cleaned up by converting it to an Excel table and following the preceding procedures. All formatting, including fonts, colors, fills, borders, etc., will remain as you left them.
Select any table design from the gallery below to apply it.
How to clean up all formatting in your table
Your table retains the format you created by hand if the previous method did not remove all the formatting.
Here's what you must do to get rid of all formatting (both preset and custom):
Select the whole table, including the headings, by clicking a table cell and then pressing Ctrl + A twice.
Select Clear ➔ Clear Formats from the Home tab's Editing group.

This results in a table losing all its formatting:

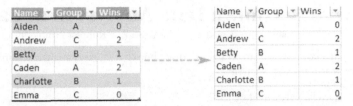

Remember that this process will remove any formatting, including alignment, number formats, and so forth.

What is the Excel procedure for disabling the table format? (Converting a table to a range)

If you find out that you no longer want tabular data, you can easily convert it back to a conventional range of cells by following these steps:

Just right-click on a table cell and choose the appropriate options.

Convert your table to the range by selecting Table ➜ Convert to Range from the menu appears.

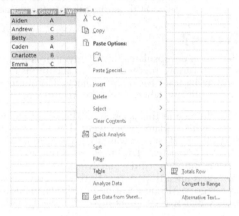

If you wish to change the tables to a standard range, you'll get a confirmation message; click Yes.

Because the table-style formatting is maintained, the final product will still appear like a table. But from the practical standpoint, it's just a regular old range; none of Excel's fancy features like structural references, auto-expansion, built-in filters, etc.

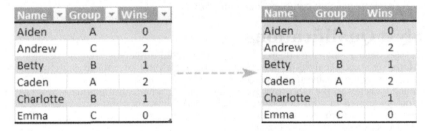

That's the procedure for erasing Excel table formatting. Some of these tidbits of advice may be useful to you.

17.8 How to Remove a Table in Excel?

If you don't need the tables in your Excel sheet anymore, here's how to get rid of them. Select all the cells to clear the table, then click the Clear button.

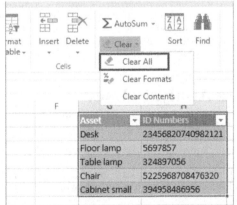

Optionally, you may highlight the table and hit the Delete key.

You can't save the information using Excel Online while removing the table structure.

Chapter 18: How to Become a Data Analyst in 2022?

If you're thinking about making a career change into data science, here are five things to think about.

- Get a four-year degree in a computer or math science discipline that stresses analytical thinking and statistical methods.
- Obtain Valuable Experience in Data Analysis
- Think About Accreditation
- Find an entry-level position as a data analyst.
- Focus your graduate studies on data analysis.

18.1 What Does a Data Analyst Do?

A data analyst is tasked with gathering, cleaning, and analyzing massive amounts of data using statistical methods. They learn to utilize data to find insights and make decisions. Advances in computing power and the trend toward more technological integration have led to new data analysis methods. Data analysts were given a new lease of life with the advent of the relational database, which enabled them to access data from databases using a language called SQL (short for structured query language).

18.2 What Is Data Analytics?

Data analytics is a vast discipline, and its definition encapsulates this by saying it is the act of analyzing raw data to uncover patterns and answer questions. Contrarily, it encompasses various methods used to accomplish various ends.

Some aspects of the data analytics method may be used for many projects. Combining these elements into a comprehensive data analytics project can let you see where you currently are, where you've been, and where you ought to go next.

- Descriptive analytics is sometine the 1st step in this approach. The act of elucidating a dataset's long-term tendencies. The primary goal of descriptive analytics is to explain "what went down." Traditional metrics like return on investment are commonly used for this purpose (ROI). Each sector will employ a unique set of metrics. Predictions cannot be made, or choices directly influenced by descriptive analytics. The emphasis is on providing a descriptive summary of the data.
- Advance analytics is the next crucial component of data analytics. In this subfield of data science, cutting-edge software is used to extract data, create forecasts, and unearth patterns. Both conventional statistical methods and modern-day machine learning techniques fall within this category. Machine learning methods, including neural networks, NLP, sentiment analysis, and others, are required to do complex analyses. This data-driven knowledge offers a fresh perspective on "what if" scenarios; advanced analytics has you covered.
- These methods are being applied to many fields thanks to advances in machine learning, the availability of large data sets, and low-cost computation. Obtaining large data sets is crucial for the development of such methods. Thanks to developments in parallel computing and inexpensive computing power, organizations can use big data analytics to derive useful conclusions from diverse and complex data sources.

18.3 Data Analyst Qualifications

To work as a data analyst, you need a bachelor's degree from an accredited university, a grade point average of at least 50%, and a background in IT, CS, Math, or Stats. Analysts in this field sift through piles of data in search of actionable insights about the company's stakeholders and methods for using that data to solve issues.

Any of the best Data Science Colleges in the US provide excellent undergraduate and graduate programs in Data Science and Data Analytics that may help you get started in your new career as a Data Analyst. In addition to meeting the educational requirements, applicants should be proficient in mathematics, have a working grasp of a programming language (Python, SQL, or Oracle are all good choices), and can analyze, interpret, and model data.

18.4 Data Analyst Responsibilities

Jobs within data analytics often include collecting and sifting through data to reveal patterns and gain business insights. What a data analyst does daily might vary widely according to the organization they work for or the field of data analytics they choose to focus on. Using tools like Tableau, business intelligence software, and programming, data analysts, could be responsible for establishing and managing relational databases and systems used by several departments within a company.

Typically, data analysts collaborate with IT departments, upper management, and data scientists to establish business objectives. They collect and organize information from new and old sources and use established statistical methods to evaluate and interpret the findings. They can often uncover new avenues for process improvement by seeing trends, correlations, and patterns in large data sets. In addition to analyzing data, analysts must document their results in reports and share their recommendations for moving forward with important stakeholders.

18.5 What Tools Do Data Analysts Use?

In addition to these primary resources, data analysts also rely on the following:

Google Analytics (GAs): With the aid of GA, analysts may make sense of consumer data like as patterns and weak spots in the user experience on the landing pages and calls-to-actions (CTAs)

Tableau: Analysts utilize tableau to compile and examine data. They may make visualizations and share them with other team members on a dashboard.

Jupyter Notebook systems: Thanks to Jupyter notebooks, data analysts may easily run tests on their programs. The markdown functionality of Jupyter Notebooks makes for a straightforward interface, which is why many people outside the technical community use them.

GitHub: GitHub is a web service for collaborating on software development projects. Object-oriented programmers and data analysts cannot do without this.

AWS S3: Cloud storage is what AWS S3 is all about. It's useful for data scientists to archive and access massive databases.

18.6 Data Analysts Job

Data analysts in the modern day need to be adaptable. The work of an analyst now requires a wider range of skills than ever before. Modeling & predictive analytics are tools used by seasoned analysts to draw conclusions and plan the next steps. Then, they face the daunting task of explaining their findings to rooms full of bewildered laypeople. They need to undergo a metamorphosis from data analysts to data scientists.

There will be a 22% increase in demand for market research analysts.

There will be 14% more demand for management analysts and other roles that rely on external links.

Data from the Bureau of Labors Statistics show an increase in employment opportunities at a rate much higher than the national average at this link: open in new. Because data analysts are useful in many sectors, including business, healthcare, IT, manufacturing, consulting, and retail, more and more careers are being formed because of technological advancements. Data is being gathered at every turn; once organized, it may be used for predictive analysis, which in turn helps improve human civilization.

18.7 Data Analyst Salary

Salaries vary widely depending on the variety and level of duties required. Pay is high for a professional data analyst with a data scientist's expertise.

The typical beginning pay for any data analyst is $83,750.

Data analysts earn an average of $100,250 a year.

Salaries for professional data analysts range from $118,750 and $142,500 on average.

18.8 Data Analyst Career Path

A typical Data Analyst career ladder begins with an Analyst I role, continues through Analyst II and Senior Analyst and culminates with a Data Scientist or CTO role. As a result, the employment market for data analysts is expected to expand steadily for the foreseeable future.

18.9 Is Data Analysis a Growing Field?

The demand for data analysts & data scientists is expected to increase at a faster-than-average rate, giving you more alternatives if you decide which field to enter. Employment prospects for data analysts are excellent. An increase of 15% is predicted for data analysts. Between the years 2020 and 2030. The salary range for a data analyst is wide, depending on factors such as industry and location. In 2021, data analysts made an average of $98,230 per year.

18.10 How to Become a Data Analyst with No Experience?

Advanced education or credential is out of reach for many people financially. If you need to be successful as a data analyst but don't yet have the experience or education for the job, consider the following options. If you want to be a data analyst, here's how to start.

Start with Self-Study

Knowledge is abundant and usually free on the internet. Mastering data analysis techniques on your own is an option if you're self-motivated and can put in the time and effort. Python, data visualization, R, Statistics, & SQL are all useful tools and languages to master. A Python lesson might be a good place to begin.

Try Out Data Analytics Projects

Do some practical work to put your newfound knowledge into practice. Once you've honed your technical chops, it's time to think about earning a data analyst certification or enrolling in one of these 10 top online data analytics courses. You should be able to create data projects & present your results as part of any course or certification you enroll in.

To save time and effort, it is possible to get free datasets in places like public repositories and use them to improve your interpretation skills.

Create your Portfolio

A portfolio is something you can put together after you've completed a few jobs and gained some experience. Employers looking to fill data analyst positions will want to view your portfolio as proof of your skills.

As a starting point, GitHub is excellent for presenting your work. You may get inspiration by perusing the portfolios of other professionals, and you can also use this to make contacts and obtain jobs.

Applying for Internships & Jobs

Prepare for entry-level data analyst opportunities by updating your résumé and portfolio. It would be greatest if you think about contacting the people you've met via your studies, projects, and other learning experiences. You may also locate fantastic job possibilities on job forums like Indeed.

Depending on how quickly you want to learn, you could be a data analyst in a few months. Depending on factors such as your dedication, hours put in each week, chosen educational route, and networking ability, the time it takes may range from several months to a couple of years.

Chapter 19: What Skills Should You look for while hiring an Excel Expert?

Many organizations rely on Microsoft Excel, a spreadsheet tool, to automate mundane tasks like recordkeeping, financial tracking, inventory management, and data analysis. Because of how intuitive and useful the program is in so many contexts, it has found widespread adoption across organizations. A wide range of skill levels may be required.

An advanced excel capabilities checklist will help you evaluate applicants based on your specific employment needs. However, do you've any concept of the qualifications to seek out? Which Excel skills are most in demand by employers?

Here's a brief rundown on how to find and recruit excel gurus for various positions. Let's go down the list of scenarios from the most complex to the least, discussing each in turn as you go.

19.1 For Entry Level/Administrative Jobs

Time-consuming and routine activities may be accomplished with the help of Microsoft Excel, making it a necessary skill for many administrative & entry-level positions.
When employing entry-level staff, look for the following proficiency levels in Microsoft Excel:

- SUMIFS / SUMIF
- COUNTIFS / COUNTIF
- Data Filters
- Pivot Tables
- Data Sorting
- Cell Formatting
- Excel shortcut key
- Data validation
- Workbook
- Charts & Analysis
- Managing Page Layouts

Asking applicants application-based questions that evaluate their real grasp of Excel's fundamentals is the best way to evaluate all the abilities mentioned above. In a fraction of minutes, you'll have a great idea of how they will tackle actual issues. The issue of "How to adequately check the Skills of candidates?" remains unresolved. What if someone told you that he had the answer to your question? In a word, yes.
Moreover, if you need to make a test more relevant to your position, you may add your questions to the existing pool. Experts in many different fields throughout the world collaborated to design your comprehensive test of abilities. This suggests you a great idea of the applicant's proficiency with Excel.
The following positions are also suitable for usage with this aptitude test:

- Secretary
- PA
- Office Administrator
- Admin Assistant
- Any Entry level job roles (business development, finance, data entry, accounting, etc.)

19.2 For Senior Level / Excel Specialists / Excel Experts

Despite the common misconception that Excel is only useful for keeping track of information, it can perform sophisticated data analysis and yield useful results for even the most difficult of queries with the help of appropriate use of the built-in formulas, functions, and VBA macros. Excel prowess at the expert level is often required for jobs in fields like data analysis, data research, programming, & project management.
Here is a broad list of the whole thing you need to know to master Excel at an expert level:

- Advanced Charting
- Excel Worksheets
- Functions
- Tool Bars
- VLOOKUP
- Advanced Formulae
- MATCH + INDEX
- PIVOT Tables and PIVOT Reporting
- Conditional Formatting
- Macros & VBA
- Simulations, Data Tables, & solver

This Microsoft Excel exam may also be used for the following purposes:

- Accountant
- Office Manager
- Bookkeeper
- VBA Projects Developers
- Project Manager

19.3 Business Analyst Excel Skills

A business analyst acts as a conduit of information between the company's IT department & the people who have an advantage in the company's victory. The business analyst engages in all these tasks, such as formulating the company's overall direction, developing its enterprise architecture, outlining the project's objectives and needs, and seeing fresh chances to grow the company. A business analyst's understanding of Excel's fundamentals and its more advanced features is essential for meeting all these key performance indicators.
To succeed as a Business Analyst, you must have the following Excel abilities.

- VLOOKUP
- SUMIFS, COUNTIFS
- Pivot Tables
- SUMPRODUCT
- IFERROR
- Charts and Chart Analysis
- MATCH
- INDIRECT
- MACROS
- Merge Data
- Conditional formatting
- IF Function
- Histograms
- Data Validation
- Regression
- Data Analysis

19.4 Data Analyst Excel Skills

To help organizations make well & more enlightened choices, data analysts are always tinkering with the data at their disposal. Their primary responsibilities include gathering information, assessing risk, and identifying threats to your company.
Let's examine the must-have Excel abilities for a data analyst:

- Functions for the data cleaning & manipulation: LEN, Concatenation, Find and Replace, Filter and Sort, Index Match, Conditional Formatting, Remove Duplicates, IfError, Logic Functions, Short-Cut
- Pivot Tables
- Macros
- Cross Reference Tables
- LOOKUP Functions
- Data filters
- Flat data tables
- Advanced Charts
- Graphics Data
- Data Interpretation
- Number Series
- Operators
- Worksheet

19.5 Auditor Excel Skills

An auditor is someone who examines financial documents and plans and executes audits. Under his watchful eye, all financial documents are error-free, and taxes are paid on schedule. This necessitates research into financial records, documenting of audit procedures in the form of audit work papers, and more.
These are the kinds of Excel proficiency in Auditors you should be looking for:

- Internal Audits of Inventories
- Balance Sheet Audits
- Internal Auditing
- Worksheet
- Charts
- Functions
- Operators
- Conditional formatting
- Macros
- Pivot Tables
- VLOOKUP, HLOOKUP

It may also be used as a hiring tool for:

- Audit Clerk
- Auditor Associate
- Internal Auditor

19.6 Seven Tips to Improve Basic MS Excel Skills

Excel proficiency may range from beginner to expert. Excel may be used for many tasks, from simple data entry to intricate formula analysis. It's vital to come up with a solid grasp of the subsequent Excel abilities. So that you may get a feel for how Excel might be enhanced, let's examine a few of the most fundamental Excel training concepts.
Mastering the Shortcuts

You may save a lot of time while using a computer by mastering a few shortcuts. Most internet and Computer users nowadays cannot function without a touchpad or mouse, yet you may save a lot of time by merely using the keyboard. Using Ctrl+C & Ctrl+V for copy & paste is second nature to

you. Ctrl+Z can be used to undo the most recent operation, Ctrl+PgUp can be used to move between worksheet sheets, Ctrl+A can select the whole worksheet, Ctrl+F can be used to search for objects, and Ctrl+K can be used to insert hyperlinks. The following is Microsoft's official list of keyboard shortcuts for use with Excel.

Importing Data from your Website

The time it takes to complete tasks may be cut by learning how and where to import data. To import data from a website into a spreadsheet, go to File ➜ Importing External Data & then select New Web Query. When you choose this tab, the current page's URL will be highlighted in your browser's new window. Select the desired web page, copy its URL, and paste it into the Address bar. Just hit the OK button, and the result will appear. All your information has been transferred to an Excel spreadsheet.

Filtering Your Results

Auto filtering is the most efficient method for sorting through a large spreadsheet. Use the menu options Data ➜ Filter ➜ Auto filter to do this. After selecting a checkbox, results may be narrowed to meet certain criteria.

Calculating the Sum

If you utilize Excel often, you may save a lot of time by learning to utilize the shortcuts available for common tasks, such as calculating the sum of an entire range or column of columns. After selecting the first blank cell in the column, press Alt + = to instantly insert the formula. After entering this command, use the Tab key to see the outcome in Excel.

AutoCorrect & AutoFill

You could practice typing less to minimize the time you spend inputting data into Excel. AutoFill and AutoCorrect are two tools that may help with this. Using AutoCorrect, you may be certain that errors or misspelled words will be fixed instantly. Select AutoCorrect from the Tools menu to activate it.

AutoFill is a time-saver, particularly when attempting to manually enter a numbered list. Choose Fill option from your Edit menu and then click the Series button to use it.

Display Formulas

Excel's display mode, which displays how the formulae look in the system, may be toggled between with a single keyboard. Ctrl + t will get you there. If you press this key combination once while working in a spreadsheet, Excel will show you the formulae themselves rather than the calculations' output.

Manage Page Layouts

Knowing how to adjust page layout is essential if you would like your prints to appear as well as they do on the computer. These adjustments may be made under the Page Layout menu. Experiment with layout choices like column widths, page numbers, and borders to find what works best for you.

BONUS

Thank you so much for reading my book.
I hope you enjoyed it, it was helpful and provided you with new knowledge.
I would really appreciate it if you could take just two minutes, before downloading your bonuses, to leave me an honest and positive review, maybe also with a photo or video of the book.

Click here or scan the QR Code to leave your review on Amazon US

Click here or scan the QR Code to leave your review on Amazon UK

If there's anything from the book that you didn't understand or have any suggestions to improve the book, contact me at drehergilb@gmail.com, I will reply as soon as possible.
Thanks
Gil B. Dreher

Your bonus

To make it easier and help you get started with Excel, in the best possible way, I am pleased **to give you 2 free bonuses**, **The 100+ best Ready-to-Use Templates** and a **Video Course**.

GIVE ME MY GIFTS
SCAN THE QR CODE

Conclusion

Regarding Excel, having more knowledge correlates to having more money. Excel may also be used to implement these principles. If you have an in-depth knowledge of Excel, you may be able to find employment in the analytics industry that pays well. Excel, as can be seen, may be used for a multitude of purposes. However, the highlights of this booklet were just a handful of those things. The word "excellence" may be used in various other contexts. Excel is a useful tool that makes professional work simpler. You can now finish a whole computation, regardless of whether you have a solid foundation in mathematics or statistics. These things can only be done using Microsoft Excel. Nobody wants to be the only person in the room who does not have experience with Microsoft Excel. You are welcome to begin your Excel training at any time

Students and working professionals alike could find it beneficial to their careers in various fields to get familiar with the fundamentals of the straightforward application of MS Excel. Beginners, who may not be acquainted with the more advanced capabilities of the program, are likely to emphasize the most fundamental aspects, such as rows, columns, and tables. This is because novices may not be acquainted with these characteristics. Before implementing the app into the day-to-day operations of your company, you need to have a comprehensive understanding of the platform and the benefits it offers.

The ease with which one may enter data into Excel is the greatest benefit of using that program. The Ribbon design in Microsoft Excel comprises instructions that may be followed to conduct fundamental tasks. These instructions can also be utilized to replace many of the methods for data input and analysis. The command groups and the keys that correspond to them are grouped in the tabs spread around the ribbon. Tabs are used to organize these tabs in this fashion. Selecting the proper tab may make it possible to complete tasks and choose instructions more rapidly.

In general, Microsoft Excel will assist you in manipulating, monitoring, and evaluating outcomes, making more informed decisions while saving time and money. Microsoft Excel equips you with the tools you need to complete any task, whether it be organizing your finances or contributing to a project for the business you work for. Using this program, it is possible to generate individualized spreadsheets for business, data interpretation, and multimedia statistical analysis by using pre-existing templates.

Excel is a versatile tool that may be used for analyzing data and doing what-if simulations. To compute the different scenarios, you will need to use formulas that are inside cells and take one or more input cells. Using the tools offered in the Control toolbox or the Forms toolbar may make it easier to deal with various value options and selections. If the appropriate steps are taken, adjusting these settings will make it much simpler to operate your models.

82103319R00066